Targeted Fund Raising

Defining and Refining
Your Development Strategy

JUDITH E. NICHOLS, CFRE

Bonus Books, Inc.

95   94   93   92   91   5   4   3   2   1

Library of Congress Catalog Card Number 91-77217

International Standard Book Number: 0-944496-29-6

Precept Press, Inc.
160 East Illinois Street
Chicago, Illinois 60611

First Edition

Printed in the United States of America

CONTENTS

Introduction

PART ONE: ARE YOU TRYING TO RAISE MONEY IN A
       VACUUM?
Chapter 1: Understanding the Giving Scene   5
Chapter 2: Philanthropic Trends   9
Chapter 3: Meaningful Giving   19
Chapter 4: The Dawn of the Age of Renewal   25

PART TWO: PLANNING YOUR DEVELOPMENT PROGRAM
Chapter 5: A Quick Lesson on Setting Challenging Fund
       Raising Goals   35
Chapter 6: Creating a Successful Fund Raising Board   41
Chapter 7: The Limits of People Resources   55
Chapter 8: Tracking Your Development Program   65

PART THREE: THE SYNERGISTIC CAMPAIGN
Chapter 9: Synergistic Fund Raising   77
Chapter 10: Begin by Saying Thank You:
       Donor Recognition and Acknowledgement   83
Chapter 11: Creating a "Wish List"   93

PART FOUR: FOCUSING ON YOUR BEST PROSPECTS
Chapter 12: The 70/20/10 Percent Rule   105
Chapter 13: The Affluence Explosion:
       The Real Affluents, The Real Impact   115
Chapter 14: Targeting Major Donor Dollars   127
Chapter 15: Expanding Your Results from Annual Giving   133
Chapter 16: Sowing for a "Harvest" of Bequests and
       Planned Gifts   141

PART FIVE: ROUNDING OUT YOUR FUND RAISING STRATEGY
Chapter 17: The Challenge of Corporate Giving   167
Chapter 18: The Fountain of Foundation Funding:
       Can You Get More than a Trickle?   179
Chapter 19: The Do's and Don'ts of Special Events   185

PART SIX: EVALUATING YOUR DEVELOPMENT PLAN
  Chapter 20: The Audit: An Evaluation Tool   197
  Chapter 21: Nichols' Generic Fund Raising Audit   203

CONCLUSION: Fund Raising with a Passion   217

RESOURCE BIBLIOGRAPHY   221

Introduction

TARGETED FUND RAISING: *Defining and Refining Your Development Strategy* is a companion volume to *Changing Demographics: Fund Raising in the 1990s.* Whereas *Changing Demographics* concentrates on who will be the prospects and donors in the years ahead, *Targeted Fund Raising* focuses on the development strategies that make sense today and tomorrow.

Fund raisers are hard workers putting in long hours to produce urgently needed results. We know our fellow Americans care. Some are generous. Many insist they would do more. Then, why aren't we raising more money? *Targeted Fund Raising* suggests a demographically driven, common-sense approach to working smarter, not harder.

Let me introduce you to **Judy Nichols' Fund Raising Truths**:

To raise money both effectively and efficiently you must:

- know who your current donors are

- know who your best prospects might be

- know how to evaluate the potential for fund raising from various development programs and choose your priorities accordingly

- know how to ask for money

- know how much money to ask for

Let's look at each of the fund raising truths in turn:

■ **Do you know who your current donors are?**
    Demographically—are they male or female? Young or old? Educated or blue collar? Living in the city or the country? Psychographically—do they vote Democratic or Republican? Attend the ballgame or the opera? See themselves as outgoing or introspective?

    To do a better job of cultivating, soliciting, and thanking your current donors, you need to know who they are and what matters to them.

■ **Do you know who your best prospects would be?**
    Will your organization's future donors be the same as the donors of today? Will they change? Should they change? How are you educating today's prospect to become tomorrow's donor?

    You need to decide who your best prospects are likely to be and develop a strategy to educate them into becoming future donors.

■ **Do you know how to evaluate the potential for fund raising in your various development programs? How do you set priorities?**
    You can't do everything equally well. Where should you concentrate your efforts? How should you judge the results?

    A well-planned development program is driven by the director, not driving him or her! Efforts are targeted for strategies with the greatest returns.

■ **Do you know how to ask for money?**
    Do you view yourself as offering opportunities to donors or presenting "bills"? Do you know how to use both facts and

emotion? Do you view soliciting as "begging" or forming partnerships?

We're offering our donors the chance to shape the future.
Most development officers and fund raising volunteers need to
be remotivated and reenergized periodically.

■ **Are you trying to raise too few dollars, rather than too many?**
    The Great Depression is over. The majority of our pros-
pects have no memories of bread costing five cents, houses
selling for ten thousand dollars, or being able to go to the movies for a quarter. Yet, we continue to ask for gifts of ten to
twenty-five dollars.

Today's givers know it takes more money to right the
wrongs. We lose their confidence when we offer false assur-
ances that miracles can be accomplished for pennies.

    Targeted Fund Raising is based on a series of workshops I
began providing around the United States at the request of various professional development organizations. Many, including
numerous chapters of the National Society for Fund Raising
Executives, United Way, the American Lung Association, Boys
and Girls Clubs of America, and a variety of other not-for-
profits, had—after initial presentations based on *Changing*
Demographics—asked for a workshop that concentrated on demographically driven fund raising strategies. But, consistently, I heard a complaint: "I had to write too much. Couldn't
you put this in a book?"
    The goal of this book is to give you useful information, not
pie-in-the-sky strategies that fall apart when you try to apply
them to your own organization. As development officers, most
of us have limitations to what we can do—we don't have
enough staffing, enough seed and project money, enough
volunteers—so we must prioritize the fund raising projects
upon which we choose to spend our time and efforts.
    Targeted Fund Raising was written for the seasoned devel-
opment professional looking for new ideas and motivation. It
will help those with an established program that needs to be
evaluated in terms of potential. It will be useful to senior and

mid-level fund raisers who are new to their current positions and want to move the development program along as quickly as possible. I also wanted it to be of value to those who are new to the profession and want an overview of how the components of fund raising fit together.

I hope it meets your needs.

Judith E. Nichols, CFRE
November 1991

PART I

ARE YOU TRYING TO RAISE MONEY
IN A VACUUM?

You can't raise money in a vacuum. Your organization's success in fund raising is equally affected by external and internal events.

The first step in putting together a realistic development program is to know what is happening beyond your organization. Understand and accept what is outside of your control so that you don't waste time trying to work against reality.

While the majority of *Targeted Fund Raising: Defining and Refining Your Development Strategy* is a ''how to'' book, focused on making your internal strategy effective, Part One explains briefly what's happening in your community, on a national level, and internationally.

Chapter 1 tells you about your competition: it's growing bigger and stronger. You need to understand it to tackle it.

Chapter 2 explores the likely philanthropic concerns of the years ahead. Will your organization be ''hot'' or not?

Chapter 3 explains how people's perceptions of money have shifted. You need to change your style of asking if you want increased results.

Chapter 4 discusses the dramatic demographic changes which have occurred and why they signal a change in our prospect pool.

Frances Hesselbein, formerly executive director of Girl Scouts of the USA and currently head of the Peter F. Drucker Foundation for Nonprofit Management, sums up the nineties by suggesting that not-for-profits will need to be mission-focused, value-based, and demographically driven. Part one explores these concepts.

Understanding the Giving Scene

Y*OU'RE NOT ALONE.* We've come a long way since 1955 when just over $7 billion was donated to not-for-profits. In just over thirty-five years, generous Americans have brought contributions to well over $122 billion annually.

The good news is that Americans are charitably minded. The bad news is that there are over 1.2 million active, tax-exempt not-for-profits just in the United States and, increasingly, your competition is not only local, regional, and national, but international in scope. More than 80 percent of not-for-profits made do with budgets of under $200,000.

What's your competition?

Some examples to consider:

International competition: the shifting of support towards Eastern Europe by many national United States foundations at the expense of established domestic programs. Do your needs have relevance in today's changing times?

National competition: the outpouring of support for the victims of the recent San Francisco earthquake and Hurricane Hugo resulted

---

> in a parallel dropping of support for local chari-
> ties in many communities. Are you a priority for
> your supporters?
>
> *Local competition:* Portland, Oregon—a
> city of less than 300,000—has nearly 3,000 not-
> for-profits. Several are in or starting major cam-
> paigns. What about your city or town? In
> addition to knowing the numbers, you need to
> know how sophisticated your competition's
> fund raising is and if there are any plans for ma-
> jor campaigns.

The number of worthwhile not-for-profits shows no signs
of diminishing. All will need funding; most will expand their
fund raising efforts.

*Question: How is your organization perceived against the
needs projected by others?*

How big is the contributions pie? The lion's share of contributions goes to religion (over 53 percent). The rest of not-for-
profits compete for just over half of the pie. Your piece may
amount to ''crumbs'' at the funding table.

You may need to articulate your organization's needs to fit
better with the interests of potential funders.

*Question: Can you ''shift'' your focus to put you more
strongly in line with funders' concerns?*

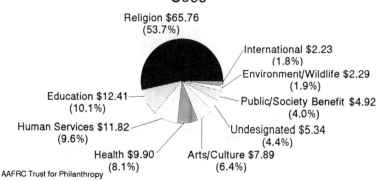

Giving 1990: $122.57 Billion

Uses

Religion $65.76 (53.7%)

International $2.23 (1.8%)

Environment/Wildlife $2.29 (1.9%)

Public/Society Benefit $4.92 (4.0%)

Undesignated $5.34 (4.4%)

Arts/Culture $7.89 (6.4%)

Health $9.90 (8.1%)

Human Services $11.82 (9.6%)

Education $12.41 (10.1%)

AAFRC Trust for Philanthropy

Who gives and why? Leaving government gifts and grants and United Way allocations aside, there are only four major sources of contribution dollars:

- current gifts from living individuals

- bequest gifts from deceased individuals

- gifts and grants from corporations and businesses

- gifts and grants from charitable foundations

Giving 1990: $122.57 Billion
Sources

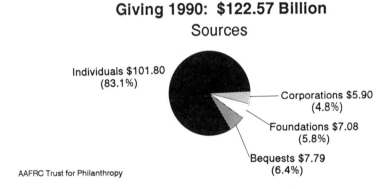

Individuals $101.80 (83.1%)

Corporations $5.90 (4.8%)

Foundations $7.08 (5.8%)

Bequests $7.79 (6.4%)

AAFRC Trust for Philanthropy

Most organizations place their efforts backwards. Boards and staff focus on the small pot of corporate and foundation dollars and ignore the broader, more lucrative opportunities of individual contributors.

The most current figures suggest some continuing trends to keep in mind when planning your development strategy. According to the AAFRC Trust for Philanthropy:

- the growth of philanthropic giving has slowed. The 1990 figures represent an inflation-adjusted increase of just 1 percent over 1989.

- gifts from individuals continue to, far and away, outdistance other sources. The most significant growth is in the area of bequests.

- foundation giving, though modest, is ahead of inflation while corporate giving is losing pace with inflation.

- gifts to groups offering services and programs in education, environmental protection, international aid and various public benefit projects rose considerably above inflation.

- giving to religion, health, human services, and the arts either declined in real terms, or surpassed inflation by less than 1 percent over the year before.

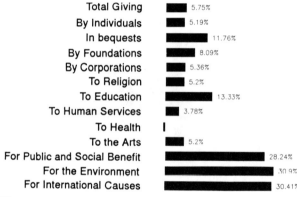

How Giving Changed in 1990

Total Giving	5.75%
By Individuals	5.19%
In bequests	11.76%
By Foundations	8.09%
By Corporations	5.36%
To Religion	5.2%
To Education	13.33%
To Human Services	3.78%
To Health	
To the Arts	5.2%
For Public and Social Benefit	28.24%
For the Environment	30.9%
For International Causes	30.41%

AAFRC Trust for Philanthropy

Corporations and foundations combined give just 10 percent of the total dollars not-for-profits receive. And increasingly, corporations and foundations prefer to give restricted dollars. For both quantity and quality (unrestricted) of gifts, look to individuals.

Question: Who are your organization's top prospects? Nine out of every ten should be individuals.

Knowing who your competition is and where the dollars are is only part of the picture. You also need to know what the philanthropic trends of the future are likely to be. We'll discuss that in chapter 2.

CHAPTER TWO

Philanthropic Trends

NEXT, LET'S LOOK AT organiza-
tional relevance. Your ability to raise money will strongly depend on whether your organization's mission, goals and
objectives become obsolete or stay relevant in the years ahead.
Do we know which services will be needed by our communities? Are we working with funders—individuals, foundations
and corporations—to strengthen the needed programs of the
future? Or, are we continuing to raise monies for projects past
their usefulness?

As we move toward the twenty-first century, key demographic trends including age, race/ethnicity, household types
and geography can help not-for-profits identify the support
services that will be needed, as well as suggest who is likely to
underwrite the cost of providing resources.*

Changing demographics will impact who will give, when
they will make gifts, how much they can donate, and what they
are likely to support. It will also determine the "relevance" of
your organization to key groupings including baby boomers,
baby busters, the emerging minority populations, a greying
America, and working women.

We are looking toward a more equal distribution by age.
Traditionally, a population has a lot of children and young

---

*In my previous books, *Changing Demographics: Fund Raising for the 1990s* and *By The Numbers: Using Demographics and Psychographics for Business Growth in the '90s* (Bonus 1990), I explore the demographic and psychographic trends in depth. Relevant reminders of key points are included throughout this book; this chapter
provides a short overview.

adults, a middling number of middle-aged people, and a small number of the elderly. But by the year 2000, we will have roughly the same number of people in each group. Eventually, because there will be fewer young people capable of reproducing, the population will begin to decrease.

Population Distribution by Age

	1980	1990	2000
Total	100.0%	100.0%	100.0%
0–24	41.4	36.0	33.9
24–29	32.7	38.3	37.6
50 +	25.9	25.7%	28.5%

Source: U.S. Census

■ **The population is aging.** The fastest-growing age groups are the oldest ones. The 1990 census shows that 57,000 Americans have reached 100—a growth of 77 percent from the 1980 census. The oldest "baby boomers" (76 million people born between 1946 and 1964) turned 40 in 1986, ushering that massive generation into midlife.

With older Americans living longer, a new wave of essential not-for-profit services is taking center stage. This includes a focus on lifelong learning, medical marvels, changes in caregiving, socialization,and financial planning.

■ **The composition of the youth population is shifting.** Youth, a smaller percentage of the total population, will be more heavily minority. The higher childbearing rates for Hispanics, blacks, and Asian Americans mean that, by the year 2010, more than one-third of American children will be minority. More children will be born into poverty than ever before.

Day care, afterschool care, camping and scouting programs will increasingly be used by a less affluent, more diversified audience. Greater family support services—parenting skills, job counseling, substance abuse, domestic violence—will also be needed.

■ **Nationwide, the number of 14- to 25-year-olds has dropped.**

The smaller cohort of "baby busters", born between 1965 and 1976, suggests, at least short-term, a smaller audience of teens and young adults. This may lead to decreased demand for programs and services associated with "Youth-at-Risk" such as substance abuse and teen pregnancy counselling. (As youth becomes increasingly minority and poor, the need for such services may—again—increase). It also means that there will be less entry-level workers, possibly fueling job opportunities for the disabled and handicapped as well as the elderly.

WHO'S WHO

Millions

Depression Births	(1930s)	33
World War II Babies	(1940–45)	13
Baby Boomers	(1946–64)	76
Baby Busters	(1965–77)	32
Baby Boomlet	(1978–)	38*

*estimated
Source: U.S. Census

The number of low-income households among this age group will decline. The biggest change forecast for this age category is that more households will have incomes between $60,000 and $75,000. But, busters embody a unique blend of economic and political conservatism while also being socially liberal. They have little interest in championing causes. However, the liberating events behind the Iron Curtain have caught their imagination. And 62 percent believe the government should make a major effort to combat race, poverty, and ghetto problems, compared to 54 percent of Americans aged 30 to 44.

■ **As the huge baby boom generation moves into middle age** during the 1990s, the nation can look forward to a drop in the use of recreational drugs, an increase in white collar crime, and an upsurge in demand for improved health care. As a "sandwiched generation,'' they will look for continuing help with childcare and increasing help with eldercare.

Will the "me" generation give? Studies indicate that a key reason boomers have been slow to contribute financially to the causes they championed in the 1960s and 1970s was due mainly to the additional time it took them to become economically assimilated. (*Fortune* magazine has estimated boomers—because of their large cohort size, competing for resources and recognition—lost 10 years of income). Middle-aging boomers *can* give.

We will also find boomers moving into positions of leadership in both corporations and foundations, directing the contribution dollars of their organizations. It's not unlikely that boomer concerns—more inner directed, with emphasis on the environment, globalism, respect for the family and human dignity—will dominate the giving scene.

Diversity is making the concept of a dominant spending group passé. The middle-income household is vanishing. Household diversity will continue to polarize incomes. However, United Way predicts that high-income households will grow faster than low-income households.

HOUSEHOLD INCOME DISTRIBUTION
1989 and projected 1994

	1989	1994
0–$9,999	9.8%	7.0%
$10,000–$14,999	5.9%	5.2%
$15,999–$24,999	13.7%	10.3%
$25,000–$34,999	13.5%	10.7%
$35,000–$49,999	18.2%	15.3%
$50,000–$74,999	19.6%	19.9%
$75,000–$99,999	9.3%	14.0%
$100,000–$149,999	7.1%	10.8%
$150,000–$199,999	1.7%	4.3%
$200,000 +	1.2%	2.4%

Source: The Affluence Report, Donnelly Marketing Information Service

■ **Hispanics and Asians will far outpace the ten percent popula-**

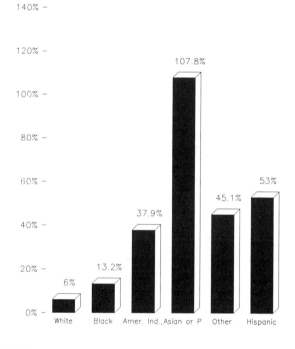

Racial & Ethnic Growth

U.S. Census

tion growth recorded since the 1980 census. The proportion of whites is declining in every age group while the number of blacks, Hispanics, and Asians is increasing.

■ **Women and minorities will be increasingly sought-after as skilled workers.** Responsibilities, occupations, and opportunities will become more alike as our society accepts diversity as a positive force.

The ability of women and minorities to support charitable causes will increase. However, our organizations will have to send a message of welcome—inclusion on boards, response to concerns, sensitivity in communications. Adapting to cultural and language differences was a major challenge in the 1980s; in the 1990s we're moving even more dramatically towards a welcoming of cultural diversity.

The traditional family continues to decline. There are more single-parent families, more couples living together without marriage, more childless adults; the 1990 census showed that the range of household types continues to broaden.

FUTURE HOUSEHOLD TYPES
Ages 35–44

As we move through the 1990s and into a new century, households will increasingly be "nonfamily" units.

	1990		2000		1990–2000
	Number (in millions)	%	Number (in millions)	%	% change
All households	21,245	100.0	24,339	100.0	19.3%
Family Households	**17,363**	**81.8**	**19,513**	**77.0**	**12.4**
Married couple	13,610	64.1	14,947	59.0	9.8
Female householder	3,083	14.5	3,632	14.3	17.8
Male householder	675	3.2	934	3.7	38.4
Nonfamily households	**3,877**	**18.2**	**5,826**	**23.0**	**50.3**
Female householder	1,351	6.4	1,806	7.1	33.7
Male householder	2,526	11.9	4,020	15.9	59.1

Numbers may not add up due to rounding

Source: The 1980 Population Survey and Bureau of the Census

■ **With both baby busters and baby boomers committed to two-career families,** time-poor families are ideal consumers for daycare (for both children and elderly parents) and organized leisure and health activities.

■ **Women have become increasingly committed to the work force and are less likely to marry and have children.** Although some marketers thought the women's labor force participation had peaked in the 1980s, *American Demographics* magazine—a respected source of trend predictions—doubts we will see a return to traditional family life.

■ **Population and economic activity will continue to shift toward the south and west.** By 2000, the Northeast will have only 19 percent of the nation's population, barely half of the South's 36 percent, according to current Census Bureau projections.

■ **More Americans will move than ever before.** Seventeen percent of us are living in a different home today than a year ago, according to the 1986 Current Population survey. Almost one in ten moves from one region to another. Young Americans move more often than older Americans.

■ **Big cities began reversing the trend of declining population that prevailed in the 1960s through early-1980s.** Most cities will *add* people over the next 10 to 15 years.

  Not-for-profits specializing in retraining of older workers, and the placement of the handicapped and disabled will find their niche.

  Let's conclude by turning to the futurists and seeing what they predict. John Naisbitt and Patricia Aburdene in *Megatrends 2000*, offer several new directions for the 1990s. The following seem to target leadership opportunities for not-for-profits:

- Renaissance in the Arts

- Global Lifestyles and Cultural Nationalism

- The Privatization of the Welfare State

- The Rise of the Pacific Rim

- The Decade of Women in Leadership

- A Religious Revival of the Third Millennium

- The Triumph of the Individual

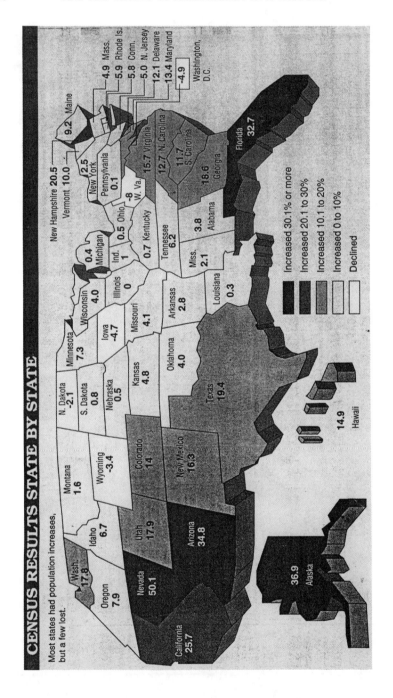

United Way's futurists suggest that there will be a revival of confidence in not-for-profit institutions. A *Business Week* feature story concurs, applauding not-for-profits as the "best-run businesses in America."

Simultaneously, Roper's *The Public Pulse* suggests that the deterioration of good will and increase of suspicion towards business will lead to massive swings in public sentiment on issues like regulation, taxation, and the environment.

This suggests an increasing number of partnerships between the corporate and not-for-profit sectors as the business community seeks charitable organizations to "put the Good Housekeeping Seal of Approval" on their activities.

In conclusion: the demographic trends we are tracking through the 1990s suggest there are five leading niches of concern for the future: dealing with the home, education, health and fitness, leisure time, and finances. All of these are areas that not-for-profits are concerned with currently. The need as we move through the last decade of the nineteenth century and into the twentieth is to take our expertise in these areas and make sure it reaches the emerging, often different, audiences who will need our services.

The challenge is also to reach out to both our traditional and new sources of funding to demonstrate how, as not-for-profits, we can make this a better world for all.

CHAPTER THREE

Meaningful Giving

THERE ARE TWO PARTS to development: the donor and the recipient. Knowing who is likely to give to your organization and what they expect from their generosity is the key to meaningful giving in the years ahead.

WHO ARE YOUR DONORS?

Do you personally remember the Great Depression? The majority of adults in the United States today were born after World War II, not before.

Ken Dychtwald, writing in *Age Wave*, suggests that "when analyzing the financial styles of any particular generation, there are two basic issues to consider: whether they have money and how they feel about spending it." Not surprisingly, most people form their core values with regard to how they relate to money during the influential years when they first start working.

■ **Older Americans still remember when modest dollars had major muscle.** Those currently 65 and older were deeply influenced in their youth by the terribly hard and financially frightening times of the Depression. Their point of view is "Save, save, save. Something terrible could happen, and you must be prepared for that rainy day."

In contrast, the next generation—those who are today in their fifties and early sixties—along with the small group born during World War II (now forty-five to fifty) were influenced by the great prosperity that followed World War II, as well as by the trying times of the Depression. Still cautious, their point of view is a blend: "Save some, spend some."

For these individuals, annual gift-giving often is pegged at twenty-five dollars, and it can be very difficult to upgrade their contributions.

■ **Younger adults anticipate higher costs for everything, from cars to contributions**. Americans born in the mid-1940s and later were fully immersed as consumers in the free-spending, affluent decades following World War II, try as their parents (and grandparents) did to inculcate in them a sense of financial practicality. Their point of view about money is thus somewhat different from that of their parents and is totally at odds with that of their grandparents. Essentially, their attitude is this: "If you have no money in the bank, but have at least two credit cards that aren't over the limit, you're doing fine."

For adults in their mid-forties and younger, you need to ask for contributions at a level that reinforces their sense of what will make a difference—a minimum request of one hundred dollars.

■ **There are more potential baby boomer donors available than all older Americans combined.** Seventy-six million Americans were born between 1946 and 1964, making them the largest generational cohort our society has ever had. Today, baby boomers form more than half the adult population—your target for current and future giving.

It makes better sense to position your requests at the one hundred dollar level rather than the twenty-five dollar level.

● **Baby boomers are capable of giving money.** Boomers are just entering their peak earning years. Landon Y. Jones, author of *Great Expectations*—the landmark biography of the baby boom, notes that during the 1990s, baby boomers will cause the number of affluent households to inflate to unprecedented heights. "The number of householders aged 35 to 54 will swell by 40 percent, from 31 million in 1986 to 44 million by 2000. Those with the highest annual incomes—$75,000 and over—

Population in Millions
(as of 1990)

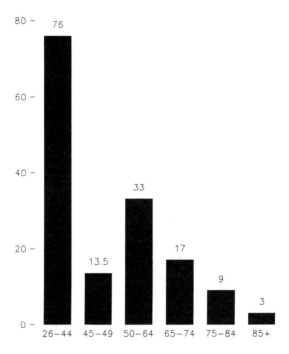

will increase from 2.2 million to 6.2 million, accounting for one in seven households in this age group by the turn of the century."

● **Baby boomers are willing to give.** In the years ahead, quality-of-life issues—making the world a better place for themselves and their children—will be the main preoccupation of baby boomers. Few boomers believe income dollars alone will improve their styles of living. They know the problems are greater than one individual or one household.

And, they want to make a difference. They know you can't save the world without spending big dollars. Asked properly, these younger, newer donors will gladly give larger dollars than did previous generations.

WHAT ARE YOUR DONORS EXPECTING FROM THEIR GIFTS?

It's been said that the heart prompts the mind to give. No matter how many "logical" reasons we can offer for gift making, most donors give because it makes them feel good to do so. To effectively raise money, now and in the years ahead, you need to look at your organization from your prospect's point of view.

Our starting point is to understand what we are "selling" to our contributors. Philip Kotler writing in *Marketing for Nonprofit Organizations* defines marketing as the voluntary exchange of benefits. To receive donations, a not-for-profit must articulate to potential contributors the benefits it provides in three key areas:

- **Addressing the donor's core need:** Each donor has an agenda s/he wants addressed. In chapter 2, I indicated that demographic trends suggest there are five leading niches of concern for Americans: the home, education, health and fitness, leisure time, and finances. These are the "core needs" of your donors.

- **Packaging the actual programs offered:** Once the individual identifies her/his core need, s/he evaluates how well various "packages" meet that need. S/he might be satisfied as easily by buying a product and/or service as by giving to charity. For example, a person concerned with combating his or her own aging might choose to buy cosmetics (short-term solution), have plastic surgery (long-term solution), join a gym, health club, or the YMCA (active solution), fund medical research (societal solution), or keep busy by volunteering (mind-over-body solution).

- **Backing up with warranties and guarantees:** Once individuals have identified the various packages that could address their core need, they analyze which path will work best for them. A product, service or organization is evaluated for credibility. Your organization's years of experience, testimonials from both recipients and donors, recognition by the community and media all provides reassurances to the donor and attest to an organization's worth.

To more effectively raise money, your staff, board and volunteers must be able to describe your organization on all three levels convincingly. This is the "story" you tell in person, on the phone, and in direct mail.

CHAPTER FOUR

The Dawn of the Age of Renewal

WHAT FUND RAISER can forget the headiness of the 1970s and 1980s? With an ever-increasing adult population to draw from, not-for-profits exceeded their development goals yearly. Acquisition was the game and fund raisers could afford to be complacent about low renewal rates. The coming of age of baby boomers gave us continuously larger pools of prospects to access. Many organizations—especially colleges and universities with "built in" constituencies of new alumni—found it easy to increase the total dollars: the same percentage penetration into a rapidly growing prospect base resulted in an increased number of gifts!

WE'VE MOVED AWAY FROM THE AGE OF REPLACEMENT

Because so much of our population was just entering its adulthood during the 1970s and 1980s, many not-for-profits had a wealth of prospects from which to choose. From the 1990s forward, we're going to have to shift our focus to retaining and upgrading the donors we already have.

As we've moved through the baby boom (those born from 1947 through 1964) to the baby bust (those born from 1965 through 1977) and into the baby boomlet (those born from 1978 through 2000), we're not replacing the high numbers of boomer births. We've dipped from 76 million down to 31 million with the bust and are looking to rebound to not more than 38 million with the boomlet.

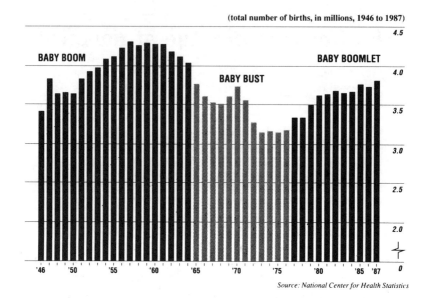

(total number of births, in millions, 1946 to 1987)

BABY BOOM   BABY BOOMLET

BABY BUST

Source: National Center for Health Statistics

Reprinted with permission ©*American Demographics*, June 1988.

You'll be dealing with the same prospects, over and over again. *Length of life is increasing dramatically even as numbers of "new" adults are decreasing.*

■ **The population as a whole is aging.** The fastest growing age groups are the oldest ones. The 1990 census shows that 57,000 Americans have reached 100—a growth of 77 percent from the 1980 census. The oldest baby boomers turned 40 in 1986, ushering that massive generation into midlife.

■ **Not only is the median age of our population moving past forty, but individuals are living longer.** "Since this century began," says Robert B. Maxwell, vice president of the American Association of Retired Persons, "there has been a 26-year gain in average life expectancy. That nearly equals the gain attained in the previous 5,000 years of human history.''

We can visualize this dramatic increase in lifespan:

1000 AD—life expectancy was 25 years

1700 AD—life expectancy was 35 years

1900 AD—life expectancy was 45 years

1980 AD—life expectancy was 75 years

1990 AD—life expectancy is 93 years

■ **The population pyramid is inverting.**

- During the 1950s–1970s, we had a large number of children and teenagers, a middling number of young-through-their-40s adults, and a very small grouping of mature adults and the elderly, forming the traditional population pyramid.

- In the 1980s through 2000, the pyramid's base of baby boomers are moving into their adult years and, as a result, the population pyramid will ''bulge'' in the middle and become a rectangle.

- And, because people can only get older, as we move into the twenty-first century, our rectangle becomes topheavy with older individuals. The population pyramid inverts.

It's no wonder that savvy marketers are already repositioning themselves to the mature market. Hallmark Greeting Cards now offers a line of birthday cards hailing the 100th year milestone!

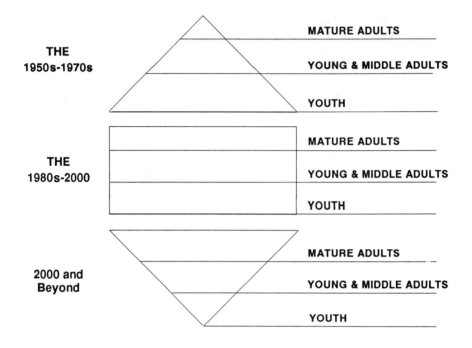

IMPLICATIONS FOR FUND RAISERS

● **How do you define a major donor?** Many not-for-profits have not stopped to think that the donor who makes a modest gift year after year, for thirty—forty—fifty years is worth treating well. A twenty-five dollar donor gives $750 over thirty years; a one hundred dollar donor gives $3,000. *You need to track cumulative giving carefully so you can share with loyal contributors your appreciation for ongoing support.*

● **Creating donor loyalty should be your priority.** Organizations will need to spend more time communicating with their donors. Newsletters, informational brochures, updates through visits, phone calls, and letters should take the place of the general fund raising appeal. *Focus on renewing and upgrading.*

Remember:

Acquisition fund raising is going to be more competitive and less productive.

A committed annual donor can continue to give, year after year, bringing the total gift-giving well into hundreds, even thousands, of dollars.

Much of the material in the following sections of *Targeted Fund Raising: Defining and Refining Your Development Strategy* follows from the implications of this first section.

Now that we've reviewed the parameters within which we do our fund raising, let's turn to strategies that maximize the results you want to achieve.

PART II

PLANNING YOUR DEVELOPMENT PROGRAM

Because raising money is a business, you need to start with a strategic plan. Knowing where you are beginning, where you are going, and what steps you will need to get from here to there, can help you avoid setting unrealistic goals and facing certain fund raising failure.

Part two of *Targeted Fund Raising: Defining and Refining Your Development Strategy* explores four crucial elements:

- Setting Challenging Goals

- Creating a Successful Fund Raising Board or Committee

- The Limits of People Resources

- Tracking Your Development Program

The starting point of a strong development program lies in setting challenging yet attainable fund raising goals. Given the needs of most not-for-profits, the saddest commentary is that many are struggling because they set their fund raising goals too low and never capture that critical combination of urgency and achievement that motivates prospects to become donors. In chapter 5, we'll discuss the key elements in goal-setting.

Next, we'll look at how you work with those good folks who give your organization its credibility. Chapter 6 explores the multiple roles of the fund raising board and volunteers: setting development goals, handling gift stewardship and accountability, and serving as your institution's advocates and fund raisers.

Chapter 7 is a reality check. Without appropriate staffing, the development office becomes crisis-driven. How can you avoid heading into burnout?

Finally, chapter 8 reviews the importance of tracking and suggests a simple spreadsheet tool you can use for defining and refining your plan. It has the benefit of being changeable, portable, and inexpensive—twelve, thirteen or fourteen-column accounting paper.

CHAPTER FIVE

A Quick Lesson on Setting Challenging Fund Raising Goals

THERE ARE TWO PARTS to goal-setting: what you need and what you can get.

<u>KNOWING WHAT YOU NEED</u>

Goal-setting starts with the board and program staff. Your fund raising goals are no more than an interpretation of what it will take in terms of dollars and donors to reach organizational, program and project objectives.

■ **In addition to deciding how much you need, you must evaluate the kinds of funding you need.** Most organizations need a mix of types of funding:

● **Unrestricted Dollars,** usually smaller gift amounts from the annual campaign, which can be used at the full discretion of the organization.

● **Designated Dollars,** of any amount, which are directed to a specific program/service area but the specific use of which is left to the discretion of the organization.

● **Restricted Dollars,** often larger contributions, whose use is fully directed by the donor.

Because few donors want their gifts to go for the mundane side of organizational life—paying for overhead and indirect costs—it is essential that you help your prospects translate such needs into fundable entities.

Chapter 11, "Creating a Wish List," describes one methodology for evaluating needs in a format that is useful for fund raising.

Most organizations need, on an annual basis, to reevaluate their needs and objectives. Short- and long-term goals need to be redefined in light of changing situations. Once the needs have been defined and given a price tag, the director of development must evaluate the *realistic potential within the donor and prospect base* to determine whether it is likely you can reach those goals or not.

KNOWING WHAT YOU CAN GET

> *A few years back I headed fund raising activities for a major organization. In one year we increased donations from $3.4 to $5.6 million. When it came time to set goals for the next year my CEO and board decided $6 million was realistic. Yet, by the end of the year, we had raised more than $10 million.*

Too often, boards and fund raisers set "safe" goals. We assume that the amount our donors are currently giving is indicative of their ability to give. And, because we don't take the time to carefully analyze what the actual potential is, we aim too low. *If we do not know (both demographically and psychographically) who our current donors are and who our best prospects are likely to be, then we may be misjudging the logical giving level.*

■ **To set challenging, yet obtainable, goals, we need to reposition our thinking.** We must focus on:

- **Output (completed solicitations) rather than input (number of prospects).** This puts the emphasis where it needs to be: on successful completions. It doesn't matter how many prospects you cultivate and solicit: it's the results that count.

- **Renewal rather than acquisition.** It's going to be more and more difficult to acquire new donors. Your best prospects are those who are already part of your "family." You need to concentrate on building donor loyalty. (This is discussed in greater detail in chapter 12: The 70/20/10 Percent Rule.)

- **Educating donors capable of doing so to give a minimum of one hundred dollars annually.** As discussed in chapter 3, the Great Depression is over! Ask for a meaningful amount. Aim at acquiring your new donors at the one hundred dollar level.

Setting challenging yet attainable goals motivates volunteers and staff to stretch, adds a sense of urgency to appeals, and increases the satisfaction that donors receive.

■ **How can you decide on your organization's challenging yet attainable goals?** By looking at your past renewal rate and seeking a realistic but attainable rate of growth. And, by making the commitment to try to upgrade *one third of your new annual donors to give at $100.*

The following is a very simple illustration of goal setting: ABC is an organization which has raised $100,000 in the previous year. It has a consistent renewal rate of 80 percent. It has 1,000 donors of under $100 with an average gift of $50.

PREVIOUS YEAR:

Major Gifts		($30,000)
($1,000 +)		
Annual Gifts		($70,000)
($100 +)	$20,000	
(under $100)	$50,000	

In setting the goals for the new year, the development director indicates his/her three priorities are:

- **Output (completed solicitations) rather than input (number of prospects).**

- **Renewal rather than acquisition.**

- **Educating donors capable of doing so to give a minimum of one hundred dollars annually.**

This translates into the following:

NEW YEAR'S GOAL: ($119,720)
  –to renew 80% with
      20% upgrade $96,000
  –to replace 20% of donors $26,720
   with modest upgrading of under-$100 donors

     Major Gifts ($1,000)   ($34,800)
     –to renew 80%
       with 20% upgrade $28,800
       ($30,000 × .80 × 1.2)

     –to replace 20%
       at current level $ 6,000
       ($30,000 × .20 × 1.0)

     Annual Gifts ($100 +)   ($23,520)
     –to renew 80% with
       20% upgrade $19,200
       ($20,000 × .80 × 1.2)

     –to replace 20% at current level
       ($20,000 × .20 × 1.0) $ 4,000

     Annual Gifts (under $100)   ($61,400)
     –to renew 80% with
       20% upgrade $48,000
       ($50,000 × .80 × 1.2)

–to replace 20% (200 donors)
    33% upgraded to $100
    (67 donors @ $100) $6,700
    67% replaced @ $50
    (134 donors @ $50) $6,700

This is a conservative scenario. It addresses renewal and replacement needs very pragmatically. Yet, the end result is a challenging yet realistic goal almost 20 percent higher than the previous year. Most importantly, it is a *logical* goal. The board and fund development committee that is shown the rationale behind the goal-setting will understand why you are aiming higher and, hopefully, will be more receptive to giving you the tools to reach your goal.

CHAPTER SIX

Creating a Successful Fund Raising Board

Y*OUR BOARD HAS THREE* fund raising roles:

- Setting and approving development goals and objectives

- Gift stewardship and accountability

- Advocacy and fund raising

Before you ask your board to raise money you must know what you are raising money for, and how you will handle the money you receive. Royster C. Hedgepeth, senior vice-president for development at the University of Colorado Foundation, notes that donors are often the last thought, if not an afterthought, when discussions of fund raising occur. Any discussion of funding must remember that donors have two basic rights:

- The right to expect that solicitations are made in the context of institutionally defined priorities.

- The right to expect that gifts will be used as the donor intended.

SETTING AND APPROVING DEVELOPMENT
GOALS AND OBJECTIVES

You can't raise money for the development department. Your donors don't see themselves as giving to the fund raising program; rather they are helping your organization reach its goals and objectives. To create a mutually beneficial relationship, your organization must be able to identify and articulate what those goals are. Unfortunately, too often, all that exists is a general catalog of needs with vague dollar amounts attached.

This requires a "bottom up" analysis. Each department or division within the organization needs to update its needs list annually.

Ongoing operating expenses, periodic capital needs, and "pie in the sky" projects should be included. The explanation of what is needed, what it will accomplish, and what it will cost must be evaluated by the organization's executive director and its board to determine priorities. The process can form the basis of a key development document, the "Wish List," described in Chapter 11.

Once the needs have been articulated, the director of development must determine the potential for raising the money. (See Part Four on "Focusing on Your Best Prospects.")

Finally, the board relying on the input from the staff, executive director, and director of development, sets the development goals and objectives. The process can take several weeks (or even months) to accomplish properly and should culminate in the setting of the development budget for the coming year.

Use an annual retreat. For many organizations, a logical "closure" to the goal setting process is to hold an annual retreat at which the ongoing board is "revitalized" and new board members are oriented as to the fund raising commitments for the coming year. This is also an opportune time to review your gift stewardship policies.

GIFT STEWARDSHIP

Donors are insisting on better accountability and stewardship from not-for-profits. Before you can go out and raise money you need to have established what you will accept and how you will handle gifts you receive. You owe that to your potential donors and to your board: accountability and stewardship are overwhelming concerns in the 1990s.

Among the questions you need to address:

- **Who can accept gifts for your organization?** Does the development officer have that right? The chairman of the board? Does it require a full board/committee meeting? You want to protect the organization: too often a donor is told immediately by a well-meaning volunteer or staffer that his/her gift will be welcome. Sometimes gifts have complications. You need to provide a "cooling off" period.

- **What types of gifts will your organization accept?** There is nothing wrong with deciding your organization has limits in terms of management and stewardship. You may not want any gifts of real estate or you may want to accept such gifts with the condition that they are put up for sale immediately. You must balance out the ability of your organization to manage long-term assets with the potential donor's needs.

- **How are you going to say thank you?** It needs to be consistent for all donors. You need to decide levels for namings, endowments, and other types of fund raising. How do you handle premiums? There's a cost involved. How much do you give back?

- **At what point do you allow restricted gifts?** As we go further up the gift-giving ladder, the proportion of gifts that come in with restrictions increases. Very few donors of one million dollars allow an organization to use their gift in any way it chooses.

- **How are operating and fund raising costs recovered from restricted and endowment gifts?** There are dozens of ways you can use to recover your fund raising costs, ranging from levying a percentage tax on all restricted gifts to using unrestricted gifts to cover costs on restricted fund raising. Once you've decided how you will do it you must communicate this information to your donors.

- **What levels of funding are required for endowments and scholarships, facility and room namings, and life income vehicles, including trusts, annuities, and pooled income funds?** It needs to be consistent for all donors: you can't "sell" the same type of room to a member of the board for less than to the general public. And, you can't be so anxious to get a gift that you accept less than is needed to handle the costs involved with the endowment's payout. It's better for everyone if the rules are set out clearly, in advance.

- **How will you handle the possibility of immediate costs involved with an endowment gift?** For example, a donor who gives you a gift of $100,000 of stock. Your financial committee decides not to sell the stock, believing the stock's value will increase substantially over the next few years. But, the donor specifies that his gift fund a scholarship of $2,000 per year beginning immediately. How will you fund this?

- **What about in-kind donations?** Do you take all that are offered? How are they valued (internally) to the organization?

Once you've formulated the initial answers to these questions you need to create a document titled "Gift Stewardship Guidelines and Policies" which is available to all concerned. You should also consider adding a line onto all your fund raising brochures and reply vehicles indicating you have a written policy for gift stewardship and offering to provide it upon request.

Patricia Lewis, president of the National Society of Fund Raising Executives, concurs that stewardship questions are an ethical concern. In addition to the questions I've outlined, she recommends deciding on your policy for sponsorship and cause-related marketing; your investment policies; use of paid versus commission-based fund raising consultants; privacy of donor information issues; and reporting of pledges and planned gifts.

Your gift stewardship guidelines will expand as your fund raising efforts grow. It's a living document that needs to be updated yearly at your board retreat to reflect the stage of your development program.

On the following pages is a set of Gift Stewardship and Accountability Guidelines suitable for a beginning development program.

"ABC ORGANIZATION"
Gift Stewardship & Accountability Guidelines

Purpose: To provide a framework for staff, volunteers, and donors that answers commonly-asked questions regarding ABC Organization's policies regarding private contributions.

1. *What types of gifts does ABC Organization accept?*

- Definitions:
  Unrestricted: gifts of any amount without donor qualifications as to use

  Designated: gifts of over $100 directed to a general program/service area of interest including _____ , _____ , etc.

  Restricted: gifts of $1,000 and greater with articulated donor restrictions as to program/service area usage within a designated area

- ABC Organization accepts gifts of cash, securities, bequests, life insurance, trusts, and annuities as well as selected in-kind and real property contributions.

- Gifts of real property (including but not limited to real estate) are reviewed by the Finance Committee. Generally, such gifts are accepted with the provision that they be sold as soon as can be arranged unless they are appropriate for use by ABC Organization.

2. *Who can accept gifts on behalf of ABC Organization?*

An outright, unrestricted cash gift of any amount may be accepted by the executive director, development staff, or members of its board.

A non-cash gift (including real property, stock, or a planned gift vehicle) or restricted cash gifts (allowed at $1,000 or greater) may be accepted by the executive director, development staff, or members of the board subject to a review by ABC Organization's Finance Committee. The review will be scheduled within a 45-day period.

3. *What forms of donor recognition are given?*

- All gifts to ABC Organization are sincerely appreciated and promptly acknowledged with a letter. Unless donors request anonymity, all contributors for the immediate past fiscal year (July 1 to June 30) are listed in an Annual Report/ Honor Roll of Donors.

- Stock gifts are attributed the median price on the day received (as determined by envelope postmark if mailed).

- Gifts of real property valued at $5,000 and greater should be evaluated by the donor's independent appraiser. ABC Organization does not assign a value for tax purposes, although it will assign a general "internal" level of gift value for donor recognition.

- Donors who contribute at the $100 and above level are considered members of the **ABC Organization's Donor Appreciation Societies:**

Contributors	$100 to $999
Patrons	$1,000 to $9,999
Benefactors	$10,000 and above
Heritage Society	Bequests and Planned Gifts

The Heritage Society: acknowledges bequest and planned gifts of any amount. To qualify, donors must indicate—in writing—that they have included ABC Organization in their wills or another planned giving vehicle. No amount need be specified. Members receive an appreciative token.

The Benefactors' Society: both one-time and cumulative giving of $10,000 and greater is acknowledged. Gifts of cash, securities, or irrevocable planned gift arrangement utilizing a bequest, trust, life insurance, or annuity is welcome.

The Patrons' Society: provides recognition to those making annual gifts of $1,000 to $9,999. Patrons receive a personalized plaque.

The designated giving levels are:

Supporting Member:	annual gift of $9,999 to $5,000
Sustaining Member:	annual gift of $4,999 to $2,500
Member:	annual gift of $2,499 to $1,000

Each spring, members of the Benefactors' and Patrons' Societies are honored at a special gathering where they receive a distinctive keepsake in recognition of their generosity and commitment.

The Contributors' Society: acknowledges yearly donors of $100 to $999. Contributors receive a certificate, updated for each continuous year of participation.

The designated giving levels are:

Supporting Member:	annual gift of $999 to $500
Sustaining Member:	annual gift of $499 to $250
Member:	annual gift of $249 to $100

4. *How does ABC Organization recover operating and fund raising costs from contributions?*

- ABC Organization raises monies on behalf of itself and its programs/services through an intensified annual appeal strategy utilizing direct mail and telecommunications as well as a major/planned gifts strategy utilizing group and individual meetings.

All costs must be recovered from the annual appeal before undesignated/unrestricted funds are used by ABC Organization.

The costs associated with major gift fund raising (gifts of $1,000 and greater) are recovered as follows:

10 percent levy for gifts of up to $100,000
5 percent levy for gifts of over $100,000

This may be recovered in any of the following ways:

with donor agreement, taken from the gift
with donor agreement, supplementing the gift
with department/program agreement, taken from another source of revenue for that area

5. *What levels of funding are required for endowments and/or scholarships?*
Ten thousand dollars is required to establish an endowment fund or scholarship. The first grant is made in July following completion of the first full fiscal year after the fund's establishment. The grant is limited to 5 percent of the interest of the proceeding year; the remaining interest goes back into the endowment to build principal as a hedge against inflation.

6. *What levels of funding are required for trusts and annuities?*
Fifty thousand dollars establishes a charitable remainder trust or annuity. Generally, these are made available to individuals age 55 or older. Up to two beneficiaries may be incor-

porated to receive payouts. The funding of the trust or annuity must be done with a vehicle which is readily liquidated prior to payments to the beneficiary(ies) commencing.

7. What are the requirements for bequest gifts?

Bequest gifts of any amount are welcome. Because it is difficult to know what ABC Organization's need may be in the distant future, donors are advised to leave bequest gifts unrestricted.

8. What kinds of in-kind donations are accepted?

A limited amount of clothing, household and durable goods, appliances, and office equipment in good/working condition is needed. In-kind gifts are assigned no value by ABC organization. It is the responsibility of the donor to do so for his/her tax purposes.

Now your board is ready to raise money.

ADVOCACY AND FUND RAISING

Thomas J. Holce, an Oregon-based entrepreneur, is a sought-after board member. The organizations he works with benefit from his clear understanding of—and willingness to accept—his fund raising responsibilities. Mr. Holce summarizes his role, thus:

- Do I understand the PLANS and PROGRAMS for fund raising?

- Do I fully understand and endorse the CASE why someone should contribute?

- Do I myself CONTRIBUTE to the fullest measure within my means?

- Do I continually offer my additions to the MAILING LIST?

- Do I assist staff in IDENTIFYING and EVALUATING

PROSPECTS—individuals, corporations, and foundations?

- Do I share in CULTIVATING key prospects?

- Do I make INTRODUCTIONS for others to make a solicitation visit?

- Do I ACCOMPANY others in solicitation visits?

- Do I write follow-up and acknowledgement LETTERS?

- Do I write PERSONAL NOTES on annual appeal letters?

- Am I prepared to make a SOLICITATION myself?

- DO I DO WHAT I SAY I WILL DO?

You shouldn't put anyone on a board who is unwilling or unable to open doors for you and to make a personal commitment. This is the rule of "give, get, or get off." Many organizations don't follow it. If you invite someone to join your board because s/he has powerful name recognition but that person is unwilling to work on your behalf, you haven't gained anything.

■ **Too often not-for-profits fail to recognize that the invitation to join the board carries responsibilities for both the organization and the potential board member.** It's an honor and a commitment to serve: both sides need to buy into the process.

Many organizations assume that their board members won't want to fund raise. And, in fact, board and potential board members may tell you that they won't or can't do it. But, often the problem is that, because the board member doesn't know enough about the organization, s/he views fund raising as "rattling a tin cup"—begging—as opposed to "creating partnerships"—advocacy. *If your organization accepts and fulfills its ongoing responsibility of providing board members with current information and tools so they can confi-*

dently tell your not-for-profit's story, most of these concerns disappear.

It's important to build funding into your budget for board training. We provide staff with ongoing learning opportunities; the same needs to be done with the board. At least twice a year you should offer a formal fund raising workshop. Use an outside trainer. Why? You're never a prophet in your own backyard: let a respected "stranger" enhance your standing by confirming the recommendations you've been stating all year long.

● **Institute a year-long nominating procedure.** Finding the best board members means doing your homework. It shouldn't be left for the last moment. That sends a signal to possible members that your organization doesn't take the board seriously. Potential board members should be interviewed well in advance of the nominating committee's deadline for recommendations. The initial interview should include a follow-up invitation to tour the agency or see a program or project in action.

● **Have a clear job description.** Potential board members should be clearly informed about their obligations in advance of accepting a term. Your job description should include the frequency of meetings, requirements for committee assignments, fund raising responsibilities, and if there is any requested level of financial contribution.

JOB DESCRIPTION
Member, Board of Directors

The purpose of the board of ABC Organization is to direct, implement, and evaluate the organization's short- and long-range strategies in support of the mission and objectives.

Each member of the board has the following responsibilities:

1. To attend the quarterly meetings of the entire board

2. To attend the necessary committee meetings with his/her area of specific responsibility

3. To become familiar with the goals, objectives, and programs/services of ABC Organization so as to become capable of being an articulate advocate of the organization

4. To be committed to the goals and objectives of ABC Organization and to be willing to make an annual gift towards support of the organization at a level which is meaningful for that individual

5. To be willing to articulate the goals and objectives of ABC Organization to those capable of financially supporting it. Each board member is expected to take responsibility for the cultivation/solicitation of three to five donor prospects in the course of a year.

● **Orient new board members before they begin serving.** Schedule a block of time prior to the start of the new term of office when—in a group—new board members can go over the by-laws and organizational structure, gift stewardship guidelines, and the budget. A suggestion: invite the current members of the board to attend if they wish (some will!) and back the session up with a "get-acquainted" luncheon or dinner for new and current board members.

• **Revitalize the ongoing board.** A portion of each board meeting should remind members why they are volunteering. Bring in a staff member to demonstrate a success, show a program in action, use tapes and slides to review a recent triumph. Hold longer training events once or twice a year. Be sure your board members understand that yours is a vibrant, dynamic not-for-profit that makes a difference in the community.

• **Use the goal-setting process to help board members understand organizational needs.** It's hard to ask for money if you don't think the organization needs it. Demonstrate the difference that dollars can make—an additional fifty children getting immunizations, an enlarged audience of disadvantaged and the elderly enjoying the pleasure of ballet, racing against the clock to find a cure.

• **Ask for the personal commitment.** Every board member should be expected to make a meaningful personal gift. (You may want to review Chapter Three on "Meaningful Giving.") Often, we neglect to ask formally for this commitment. The board's annual campaign should lead off the yearly fund raising effort. It needs to be done and it needs to be done well. If your chairman of the board and executive director don't feel comfortable setting the stage for this all-important kick-off, consider using a consultant or another volunteer.

■ **Sometimes, you have no choice.** Some not-for-profits have board structures that require representation from government agencies, civic organizations, and the populace being served. These board members may not have a personal commitment to your organization. That makes it difficult to get them to either fund raise or donate. If that is your scenario, consider setting up an ancillary fund raising council or committee. For this group, the fund raising responsibilities can be written into the job description and adhered to in choosing new members or renominating existing ones.

Remember: to raise money successfully, the executive director must furnish the vision for the organization, the director of development must handle the logistics and, if necessary, close the sale, and the board must demonstrate community support for your organization.

CHAPTER SEVEN

The Limits of People Resources

ALL DEVELOPMENT PROGRAMS have limits to their resources. In addition to finite budgets, not-for-profits tend to be lean on staffing. As you begin to build your development strategy, you must evaluate your staffing resources. Decide how to handle potential extra-time requirements.

An effective fund raising program requires adequate staffing. Rather than falling into the trap of trying to take on too much yourself and ending up burnt-out and frustrated:

- Prioritize what will be done and stick with the written plan

- Get commitments to acquiring more staff as results justify this

- Use volunteer, part-time and/or consulting help

Conduct reality checks from time to time. Set your fund raising program up to be the best it can and, equally important, respect yourself and your limitations.

USE STAFF WHERE RESULTS ARE GREATEST

Many not-for-profits use a "buckshot" approach to staffing. Rather than deciding which fund raising strategy (or strategies) make the most sense for their organization and staffing for strength in those areas, we automatically fill in every strategy area—major gifts, the annual fund, corporate and foundation relations. The result: each area is thinly staffed and the entire development program suffers.

If your staffing resources are limited, decide which area makes most sense for your particular organization and staff-up there. For many—but not all—organizations this will be the cultivation and solicitation of individuals capable of giving significant gifts. Remember:

- Eighty to ninety percent of the dollars come from ten to twenty percent of the donors

  and

- Ninety percent of giving comes from individuals

Whatever staffing scenario you decide makes sense for your organization, make sure your CEO and board understand why you're recommending it.

THE IMPLICATIONS OF A SMALLER WORKFORCE

Changing demographics are having a serious impact on who's available to work. Not-for-profits, even more so than in previous years, are finding heavy competition for both seasoned and novice staff.

In addition to the competition caused by dramatically increasing numbers of not-for-profits, labor shortages are occurring for three primary reasons:

- a dramatic decline in the available pool of traditional entry-level workers

- a restructuring of the skills required in tomorrow's workplace

- an increasing demand for college-educated workers

■ **The competition for entry-level workers is greater.** The United States is facing its first labor shortage in 20 years. Unemployment is at its lowest point in 15 years—5.2 percent. And the tiny baby-bust generation, those born between 1964 and 1975, can't possibly fill all the entry-level positions the baby boom is vacating or the millions of new jobs created each year. By 1990 the number of 18-year-olds had dropped by 8 percent, according to a Census Bureau estimate, and will not reach 1989's level again until 2003.

Because we're facing a mere 1 percent growth a year in workforce growth in the 1990s (compared to the vigorous 2.9 percent growth in the 1970s), the number of traditional entry-level workers will decline by a startling 20 to 25 percent!

Not-for-profits with traditionally low pay scales for entry-level positions will be especially hard hit by the increased competition.

■ **The jobs themselves are becoming more demanding, more complex.** While computer technology and automation have taken the physical strain and boredom out of many jobs, work has become far more mentally demanding. Employees must handle a variety of skills, make snap decisions and adapt to unpredictable changes. *The Wall Street Journal* calls this "the workplace revolution" and notes that "the new jobs involve wrenching adjustments for both managers and workers. Managers who must delegate more decision making feel threatened about relinquishing their power. Among workers, problem solving, analytical skills and teamwork are in high demand— and short supply."

Not-for-profits are routinely requiring computer literacy as well as strong oral and written communication abilities from both professional and support staffs.

■ **The demand for college-educated workers may outstrip the supply.** The U.S. Department of Labor, in a report on the employment outlook from 1988 to 2000, notes it expects the number of jobs requiring education beyond high school to rise 22 percent, compared with an overall job growth rate of 15 percent.

The Hudson Institute, in a study for the Department of Labor called Workforce 2000, confirms the growing complexity of most jobs. Below-average skills will be good enough for only 27 percent of the jobs created between 1985 and 2000, compared with 40 percent of the jobs existing in the mid-1980s. And 41 percent of the new jobs will require average or better skill levels, up from 24 percent, the study says.

Not-for-profits have, typically, requested at least a bachelor's degree for professional staff applicants. The competition will be extremely keen for the college-educated pool.

WHERE CAN YOU FIND YOUR NEW STAFF?

More and more employers are competing for the best of the workforce pool: a pool that is both changing and shrinking.

● **Women, older workers, minorities, new immigrants, the handicapped and the disabled will, of necessity, find employers more welcoming.** "In today's economy, employers can't afford to discriminate," says former Secretary of Labor Elizabeth Dole, now heading the American Red Cross. She sees the shortage of workers as an "opportunity to assist those who have been at the end of the line for far too long."

Who will be applying for jobs in the years ahead? On average, 51 out of every 100 job applicants will be women, 77 will be aged 16 to 29, 15 will be Hispanics, 13 will be non-Hispanic blacks, and 6 will be Asians.

From now until the end of the century, 88 percent of workforce growth will come from women and minorities. White males, meanwhile, account for most retirees and are leaving the workforce in record numbers. By the year 2000, white males—once the mainstay of the U.S. economy, will account for only 15 percent of new job recruits. Women will comprise two-thirds of the new workers and an additional 20 percent will be nonwhite or immigrant men.

Notes Audrey Freedman, an economist at the Conference Board in New York: "Now for every ten jobs there may be eight applicants. Four are women, and three are immigrants. Of the four young men applying, only two are white, and one may take drugs."

BUILDING EMPLOYEE LOYALTY

Keeping productive employees should be a top concern for not-for-profits considering the fact that the average American worker has held eight jobs by the age of 40, according to a study released by Western U.S. Lifesaving Association.

A Gallup survey shows that members of the post-war generations who entered the work force since the 1960s are significantly less satisfied with their jobs than older Americans. Whereas only one in four (24 percent) of workers between the ages of 18 and 49 are completely satisfied with their jobs, the rate of comparable satisfaction among older workers is nearly double.

■ **Not-for-profits have a built-in appeal for baby boomers and baby busters.** *The Chivas Regal Report on Working Americans* indicates that highly-educated baby boomers want to contribute to the public good. One in three (33 percent) of this group say the desire to contribute to society is a key priority for them, compared with 15 percent of other working Americans.

■ **Marketing your business to potential workers is the key to surviving the worker shortage** says John Mancuso, a senior consultant at the Wyatt Company's Boston office. "Anyone can put a help-wanted ad in a newspaper," he says. But to compete effectively against other businesses, "employers must evaluate what benefits appeal to their target labor pool, and then find cost-effective ways to offer these benefits."

■ **Providing Employee Assistance Programs that resolve problems** can keep a valued employee on the job. Not-for-profits have often justified lower salaries by pointing to the benefits they provide to employees. Today such programs range from encouraging workers to stay healthy by providing fitness programs at the workplace to offering or identifying services for resolving problems with substance abuse, child and elder care, family conflict, finances, legal matters, and organizational conflict.

Tuition-assistance programs, job sharing, employee savings plans, and four-day workweeks are some of the "bells and whistles" employers should consider, says Mancuso.

● **Childcare: the outstanding employee benefit of the nineties.** In a world where most women work, the separation between work life and home life has become less distinct. Problems once handled at home are invading the workplace, because there may be no one at home to take care of them. Not-for-profits—with a heavily female workforce component already—will be under greater pressure to offer day-care benefits, as well as part-time and flextime hours, to attract and retain women as well as men.

● **Eldercare: the growing concern for the future.** Today there are approximately 30 million elderly persons in the United States representing more than 12 percent of the population. By the year 2030 it is projected that there will be 65 million elderly people or 21 percent of the American population. With this rapid expansion of the elderly population in our country, we can anticipate that increasing numbers of employees will be faced with the responsibilities of working and taking care of an elderly relative or friend at the same time.

Since providing care for aged relatives or friends can often be an emotional and financial drain on employees, your organization can expect to be directly affected in terms of decreased productivity and quality of job performance. Not-for-profits need to think about ways in which they can assist employees who are coping with elder care responsibilities.

● **Helping the "sandwiched" employee.** And, 5 million Americans (typically, a female age 53, but increasingly a baby boomer) can already be classified as members of the "sandwich generation," caught in the squeeze between caring for children and dependent parents, and their numbers are increasing steadily as medical technology keeps more Americans alive longer.

For women handling the needs of an aging parent or parent-in-law in addition to caring for children, the strain can be terrible. Many switch to part-time jobs, pass up promotions or quit their jobs altogether.

■ **Cultural diversity is a fact of life in today's—and tomorrow's —workplace.** Diversity can bring innovation, creativity, and better problem solving. A culturally sensitive, diverse work force enables organizations to better understand and serve its equally diverse customers and consumers. But the benefits are not automatic: tensions among employees lower productivity and create high costs in employee absenteeism, turnover, EEO and harassment suits, and unrest. And failure to understand cultural differences can lead to misunderstandings, poor performance, and unwise hiring and firing decisions.

● **Diversity has to be deliberately well-managed.** The future success of American enterprise, in both the public and private sectors, will depend largely on how well employment and management policies accommodate a diverse labor pool.

● **Valuing diversity is a new concept, not merely new words for equal employment opportunities or affirmative action,** insists the wife/husband team of Lennie Copeland and Lewis Griggs, who are producers of a film/video series which shows specific situations which cause conflict and poor performance, and how such situations can be better handled.

> Valuing diversity means recognizing and appreciating that individuals are different, that diversity is an advantage if it is valued and well-managed, and that diversity is not to be simply tolerated but encouraged, supported and nurtured.
> Valuing diversity is a state that reflects a point of view, an attitude, a purpose, and actions that are essentially different from EEO or affirmative action.
> Valuing diversity looks at the multicultural workforce from a positive perspective rather than from a defensive position.

According to Copeland, many EEO and HRD professionals seem to agree that five major problem areas need attention:

● stereotypes and their associated assumptions

- actual cultural differences

- exclusivity of the "white male club" and its associated access to important information and relationships

- unwritten rules and double standards for success which are often unknown to women and minorities

- lack of communication about differences

The *Valuing Diversity* training materials assert that overcoming these barriers to valuing diversity requires specifically addressing each problem through a clear plan of action. Copeland says that managers need to:

- recognize the assumptions they make and how these affect decisions; avoid letting stereotypes interfere with valid assessments and good judgment.

- invite outsiders into the "club" and provide employees who are different with what they need to succeed: access to information and meaningful relationships with people in power.

- teach the unwritten rules to those who need to know them. And change the rules when necessary to allow diversity to benefit the organization.

- encourage constructive communication about differences.

- treat people equitably but not uniformly. Build on individual differences. Value diversity.

Move your organization toward the future, don't resist it.
As former Xerox Chairman David Kearns says, "Understand

that over the long term, the successful manager is going to have to deal with large numbers of minorities and women in business, and I presume most managers want to be successful, want their company to be successful. Therefore, don't walk away from it; walk up to it.''

CHAPTER EIGHT

Tracking Your Development Program

THE CHESHIRE CAT may have said it best: if you don't know where you're going, any path will do. To raise money successfully, you need to choose the right development roads to follow. And, once you've decided on your strategy or strategies, you'll need to monitor your progress. This chapter shares a simple but effective tracking tool.

■ **A tracking system should enable you to visualize all the elements of your development program at once.** A good development program is complex, requiring the development officer to balance many elements at once. It's similar to being an orchestra conductor. And, in one-person shops and smaller organizations, you will also play the violin and beat the drums!

● **A fund-raising tracking system should monitor "related" activities.** You also need to track membership/alumni affairs, public relations, publications, imaging, board relations, volunteer relations and community outreach. The CEO being approached for a corporate gift may also be an alumnus you have targeted for a major personal gift. S/he should be invited to special events, receive your newsletter, and be encouraged to volunteer as well. Deliberately building *synergies* (a concept described fully in Part three) will add strength and reach to your fund raising, expanding your cycle of cultivation and solicitation.

The savvy development officer tracks what is happening in areas impacting on fund raising whether or not s/he has direct responsibility for these areas.

- **Your tracking system handles several needs at once:**

    - Provides a *timeline* of what is happening so you can prevent "slippage" as deadlines are missed

    - Alerts you to *overlappage* among programs so your prospects don't receive four pieces of mail on the same day

    - Identifies *opportunities* for using a related vehicle, saving time, money and energy

    - Warns about *overloading* staff and volunteers because of unrealistic scheduling

    - Creates a *preliminary strategy and budget* for the coming year

    My favorite planning tool is accounting paper. For less than five dollars, you can buy a pad of fifty sheets. It provides a visual reminder of where you are in an easy, inexpensive format. Not only is it less expensive than the large, formal charts that are sold, using accounting paper encourages you to take your planning with you at all times and to make changes as often as necessary. It comes in twelve, thirteen and fourteen-column formats: any version will work.

- **Creating a tracking document is easy.** Down the left-hand side of the paper, place the elements of both your development and related programs. These should include (but aren't limited to):

DIRECT FUND RAISING

- Annual Giving
  - face-to-face
  - group
  - direct mail with phone follow-up
  - phone alone
  - direct mail alone

- Major Giving
  - face-to-face
  - group

- Planned Giving
  - bequest marketing
  - financial planning workshops
  - appointments

- Corporate Relations
  - contributions
  - sponsorship/marketing

- Foundation Relations
  - grant-writing

- Special Events
  - friend raising
  - fund raising

RELATED TO FUND RAISING

- Communications Vehicles
  — annual report
  — newsletter
  — annual meeting
  — advertisements and/or public service
    announcements

- Membership Programs
  — ongoing
  — one-time

- Board and Volunteers
  — regularly scheduled meetings
  — retreats and training events

Along the columns, left to right, put the months of your fiscal year. If it runs January through December, start at column one with January and end in column twelve with December. (If you are using thirteen- or fourteen-column paper, you can use the extra columns for one month's pre- or post-fiscal year planning.)

■ **Your first attempt at tracking requires five steps:**

One: Record a historical summary of what your program has been all about.

Two: Chart out your plans for the current fiscal year on a separate sheet.

Three: Flesh out the current fiscal year by charting separate sheet(s) for each methodology if complex.

Four: Begin to chart the next fiscal year, adding ideas as they occur.

Five: Flesh out the next fiscal year by charting separate sheet(s) for each methodology if complex.

● **One: Record a historical summary of what your program has been all about.** Go back to the last complete fiscal year and record what actually took place. Under direct mail, for example, you might have sent out a March mailing of 5,000 to former donors and a November mailing of 10,000 to your entire prospect list.

● **Two: Chart out your plans for the current fiscal year.** Depending on when you first use this charting procedure, some of your entries will record events and programs which have occurred already, while some of your entries chart events and programs still to come.

● **Three: Flesh out the current fiscal year by charting separate sheet(s) for each methodology if complex.** Many of your development plans have multiple steps. A direct mail piece, for example, does not simply appear ready for mailing. You need to conceive the theme, write the copy (or have it written for you), have the piece printed, and—finally—have it mailed. Identify the programs and events on your summary tracking sheet which are your responsibility. Recreate a timeline for those which have occurred and put a timeline in place for those still to come.

It helps to use different colored inks to represent different steps: i.e., red for creative time; blue for printing; green for mailing.

● **Steps Four and Five: Begin to chart the next fiscal year, adding ideas as they occur. Flesh out the next fiscal year by charting separate sheet(s) for each methodology if complex.** Most organizations leave the planning process until too late. Then, they must "guess" at the expense budget the development strategy will require. The advance tracking sheets you prepare under steps four and five can give you a significant head start.

199—

Sept Oct Nov Dec Jan Feb Mar April May June July Aug

Direct FR
Annual Giving
  face to face
  group
  direct mail/phone
  phone
  direct mail

Major Giving
  face to face
  group

Planned Giving
  request mktg
  workshop
  appointments

Corporate Relations

Fdtn Relations

Special Events
  fund raising
  fund raising

Related to FR
Communications
  annual report
  newsletter
  annual mtg
  adv/PSA

Membership programs

Board/Vol
  meetings
  retreats

Tracking "rolls over" in year two. You will always need the same five sheets to be able to compare the historical, the current, and the future. But in your second year, you will have three of the sheets (steps one, two, and three) already prepared.

Don't hesitate to make corrections. The beauty of using accounting paper rather than a more expensive tracking board is that you can make changes—over and over again—easily and inexpensively. This encourages flexibility in your thinking.

PART III

THE SYNERGISTIC CAMPAIGN

Targeted Fund Raising takes a holistic view of fund raising, emphasizing ways you can make the whole program stronger than its individual parts. Part Three explains the concept of the Synergistic Campaign and introduces its key components.

Chapter 9 concentrates on the overall concepts of synergy and offers ideas on how to structure your development program so each part enhances the whole.

Chapter 10 builds on a key premise introduced in chapter 4: that the age of acquisition has turned into the dawning of the age of renewal. Because fund raisers will be focusing on the same prospects and donors, the key element in the cultivation/solicitation cycle will be how you say "thank you." Donor recognition impacts on your efforts to educate donors to give at the one hundred dollar and above level and is a key to formulating donor loyalty. Included is a complete discussion of the elements of a donor recognition program with illustrations you may adapt for your organization.

We'll close with a discussion of the "Wish List," a valuable means of enabling your organization to better communicate with its various constituencies while educating them as to your needs in an attractive format. **A Wish List brochure** helps explain who your organization is and what it does by providing donors and prospects with specific examples of products and services which enable your organization to continue and expand its help to the community. Included are the names, descriptions, and costs of tangible items. Intangible items are described as well, in a way that makes them tangible! It encourages giving from both individuals and organizations; small gifts and large; current and deferred giving. Chapter 11 describes this very important concept.

Synergistic Fund Raising

ONE OF MY FAVORITE concepts is **synergy**. Webster's Dictionary defines this as being "the working together of two muscles." In fund raising, this often translates into understanding that various development vehicles and methodologies must "mesh" if the whole is to be greater than its parts.

Each aspect of a development program affects other parts. A strong development program must be balanced. Think of a stool: if you cut one leg off, it tips; conversely, if one leg is too long, it topples. The same reasoning applies to your fund raising. Each element must balance the others and all must progress at a consistent, steady rate.

Most prospects have a variety of "pockets" you can access. Giving to the annual fund does not disqualify a prospect from also making a bequest, sitting on the charitable gifts committee of the local foundation or corporation, and attending special events. Your best donors will tend to be your board members and volunteers; readers of your newsletters and magazines; and those who make use of and/or recommend to others your products and services. Therefore, even as you are directly appealing to a prospect for one type of gift, you should always be setting the stage for other activities as well. *This is synergy.*

You can create synergies by having each fund raising and organizational vehicle serve a variety of purposes. Your newsletters and other communications vehicles, for example, should always carry articles or ads on bequests and planned gifts; your special events should be an umbrella for different types of gift-giving and revenue opportunities from "patronage" to "underwriting" to "advertising" for both individuals and organizations. In Parts four and five, as we review the various fund raising strategies, you will notice many recommendations that promote the concept of synergistic fund raising.

Once you consciously concentrate on creating synergies in your fund raising, you'll find numerous opportunities to do so in your various vehicles and activities. You'll save money and increase your outreach.

Synergistic Fund Raising for Individual Prospects

Throughout *Targeted Fund Raising* I keep emphasizing and re-emphasizing the importance of focusing your fund raising on individuals rather than corporate and foundation prospects. Too often, however, we don't use a synergistic fund raising strategy in dealing with our prospect pool of individuals.

There are three levels of individual prospects:

- Major Gift Prospects capable of making gifts at the very top of the giving pyramid.

- Affluent Prospects capable of making annual gifts of one to several thousand dollars.

- Broad Base Prospects capable of ongoing smaller gifts year after year.

■ **Your fund raising methodology must match your prospects.** You want to deal face-to-face with your most major prospects and step it down, one prospect at a time, to less effective strategies. To do this, you must know who is capable of making a large gift. Strong prospect research is essential. Essentially prospect research is of two types:

- Demographic and psychographic research to alert you to potential either within your broad prospect base or to locate populations similar to the donors you already have.

- Indepth research done on an individual to enable the development team to better cultivate and solicit.

■ **Prioritize the prospect pool of individuals and choose the appropriate methodology for reaching these persons.** We use the more effective but time intensive face-to-face cultivation for the smaller group of individuals likely to give large current and/or deferred gifts and rely on direct mail and phone contact to reach the greater numbers of prospects whose gifts will be smaller.

You must decide where the "breaks" come in your development strategy: at what point must you move from one methodology to another. Given your volunteers' willingness to do face-to-face cultivation and solicitation, your staff's sophistication, your CEO's availability, etc.—how many individuals can you realistically approach face-to-face before turning to less effective but less time-intensive vehicles? *Because most not-for-profit organizations do not decide, logically, on how many prospects they can handle at each step, they have large numbers of better prospects who are consistently ignored.*

The continuum (from most to least effective) might be described thus:

TOTAL PROSPECTS POOL (HOW MANY?)	NUMBER OF PROSPECTS	METHODOLOGY
Face-to-face		
Assign 3 – 5 prospects to each solicitor	1. Number chosen limited by your volunteer/staff willingness and availability	One-on-one may require several repeated meetings with each prospect
5 – 10 prospects at a time. Schedule regularly.	2. Larger number can be invited but scheduling is more complex	Group lunch, dinner followed by one-on-one appointments or phone contact
GOAL: Focus on outputs rather than inputs. Ask volunteers to commit to successfully completed cultivations/solicitations rather than numbers of prospects.		
Telecommunications and Telemarketing		
Limited by your logistics (phone lines available/callers you have)	3. Larger number can be reached but cost (as a %) is much higher	Combination of Direct Mail (cultivation) and Phone (solicitation)
Limited by your logistics (as in 3)	4. Larger number Poorer fulfillment	Phone calls alone
GOAL: Renewal and upgrading. Educating donors to give at the $100+ level of support.		
Direct Mail		
Limited by your knowledge of base and computer capability	5. Larger numbers Poorer fulfillment	Personalized
Limited only by budget	6. Largest numbers Poorest response	Non-personalized
GOAL: Acquisition of new donors, ideally at the $100+ level of support, but—primarily—to keep the donor base expanding.		

Working through the "breaks" of your fund raising strategy helps you prioritize. You'll be able to decide, more logically, how many staff and volunteers and how much of your budget should be expended at each level. You'll find yourself allocating the larger chunks of time to the more productive areas as well.

CHAPTER TEN

Begin by Saying Thank You: Donor Recognition and Acknowledgement

GIFT ACKNOWLEDGEMENT and recognition both closes the cultivation cycle and opens it again. Too often, we don't pay as much attention to the contributors we already have as we do to the prospects we hope to acquire. *Smart not-for-profits concentrate their efforts on retaining, renewing, and upgrading the donors they already have.* Therefore, the right place for starting your development program is with a strong donor recognition and acknowledgement program.

DONOR ACKNOWLEDGEMENT

■ **All gifts should be promptly and gratefully acknowledged.** Don't try to save money by not sending a card or letter of appreciation to your lower-level donors; instead view them as your best source of larger gifts and bequests and treat them accordingly. Not only should you send an attractive acknowledgement, you must send it immediately upon receipt of the gift. *All gifts should be acknowledged within two weeks of receipt.*

■ **Use the acknowledgement process to educate donors.** Enclose a photograph. Cite an example of how the gift will be used. Have a student or client tell, in his/her own words, what your organization means to him/her. Attach a positive press clipping. Share good news about goals met, kudos awarded.

■ **All gifts are not the same.** Depending on the number of donors
your organization has and the staffing (paid or volunteer) you
can call upon, you must decide how much personalization you
will bring to the acknowledgement process. You may want—as
part of your gift stewardship and acknowledgement
guidelines—to differentiate between the effort (and expense)
you give to a one dollar donor and a one hundred dollar donor.
Recognizing the latter is the role of a formal **donor recognition
program** discussed later in this chapter.

ANNUAL HONOR ROLL

Don't be stingy with your thanks! Too often, not-for-profits decide to save a few dollars by restricting listing in an honor roll
to the few major donors. Even worse, some organizations ignore *all* contributors by not listing any donors at all.

This really doesn't make sense. If your goal is to create ongoing donor loyalty so you can count on gift after gift, time after time, you need to demonstrate your organization's
appreciation. You should look for *more rather than less* opportunities for saying thank you.

With that in mind, consider doing a "running honor roll"
by listing early contributors in your first newsletter of the fiscal
year; adding new names in which subsequent issues; and
printing the full list immediately after the close of the fiscal
year. In addition to demonstrating to "early birds" that their
support is truly appreciated, this concept allows you to make
corrections on an ongoing basis so your final honor roll document is nearly perfect.

In addition to your letters of appreciation and an annual
honor roll listing of donors, you should develop a structured
donor recognition program for those who give one hundred
dollars and above. The rest of chapter 9 describes the elements
of such a program in detail.

DONOR RECOGNITION PROGRAMS

Correctly positioned, your donor recognition program provides both recognition for current gift-giving and education

for future gift-giving. It tells your donors you appreciate what they have done but it also lets them know more is needed.

The emphasis must be on the intangible rewards of belonging. Very few not-for-profits can afford—either financially or ethically—to offer premiums that use up a large proportion of the gift made. For this reason I prefer to call donor recognition programs **Leadership Societies**, rather than gift clubs.

There are many key phrases you can use in your letters of invitation, brochures, and other promotional vehicles to signal members and potential joiners of the Societies' role in your organization. I have used the following:

- "A natural gathering of those who provide leadership to our organization"

- "Saluting individuals who, through their substantial contributions to our organization, show a deep interest in our work"

- "Thanking those who, by example, encourage others to support our efforts"

- "In appreciation to men and women of vision"

- "To thank those who create the margin of excellence"

● **Who qualifies for Leadership Societies?** All donors who give above your minimum qualifying level. They are automatically enrolled and are informed of this honor through various Leadership Society documents described later in this chapter.

● **Do donors upgrade because of the Leadership Societies' recognition?** Jerry Panas, writing in *Mega Gifts*, reconfirms that the number one reason donors give is because of a belief in your organization. It is unlikely that large numbers of individuals will choose to give to your not-for-profit for recogni-

---

Mega Gifts, by Jerry Panas, is available from Precept Press, 160 E. Illinois St., Chicago, IL 60611. $34.95.

tion alone. But the recognition you provide is the "glue" that bonds your donors more securely to your organization. It demonstrates your recognition of their importance and helps build ongoing loyalty by providing opportunities for the donor to learn more about the difference they make.

And, while the majority of members will qualify because of the gifts they have chosen to make, others will choose to make their gifts *at a particular level* because of your Leadership Societies. These individuals will tend to have more outer-directed personalities: they are concerned with being part of the "in" group; they look for signals that neighbors, friends, and colleagues are at parity in gift-giving; they need to belong. These individuals like continuity and will give year after year. For outer-directed donors, the annual recognition devices *are* important. They want to demonstrate the ongoing nature of their support and don't like gaps. They display the plaques from every year through the present. Outer-directed donors are especially prevalent at the lowest steps of your Leadership Societies.

MEMBERSHIP STEPS FOR A DONOR RECOGNITION PROGRAM

• **Your donor recognition program should start at one hundred dollars.** And your program should encompass both annual and cumulative milestones as well as future gifts through bequests and planned giving vehicles. By doing so you continue to educate donors and prospects that

- $100 is a realistic level of beginning gift-giving and

- donor loyalty is rewarded

• **The beginning steps need to be fairly close together** so your donor does not find upgrading from one society level to another to be beyond his/her capacity. The upgrades between $100 and $999 are harder to achieve than increases from $1,000 on.

● **Even though your largest donors may be giving modest amounts you need to set the stage for more significant gifts.** One of my board members insisted on a Million Dollar Society when our premier donor was giving just $25,000. He understood we should aim for the possibility, not limit ourselves to the reality.

I recommend the following steps for all organizations:

ABC Society ($100 – $999) — This acknowledges annual giving

Member: $100 – $249
Sustaining Member: $250 – $499
Supporting Member: $500 – $999

DEF Society ($1,000 – $9,999) — This acknowledges annual giving

Member: $1,000 – $2,499
Sustaining Member: $2,500 – $4,999
Supporting Member: $5,000 – $9,999

GHI Society ($10,000 +) — This acknowledges both annual and cumulative giving

Heritage Society — This acknowledges bequests of all amounts

You can vary your second tier of annual giving and your annual/cumulative giving tier to fit your organization. If, for example, you already have one donor at the $25,000 level, you might want to have categories of annual giving within the DEF Society go from $1,000 to $24,999 and position the GHI Society at $25,000+ for both annual and cumulative giving.

MATERIALS FOR A DONOR RECOGNITION PROGRAM

You will need the following materials for a comprehensive Donor Recognition Program:

THE BASICS:

Letterhead and Envelopes
An Explanatory Brochure
A Standardized Reply Vehicle
Personalized Letters of Appreciation

ENHANCEMENTS:

Incentive Premiums
Acknowledgement Vehicles

■ **The Basics**

● **Letterhead and Envelopes** can set the Leadership Societies apart from your general solicitation efforts. By sending all correspondence from your organization to members on Leadership Society letterhead, you indicate your recognition of the role they are taking. The design need not be elaborate, but should indicate the Leadership Societies title(s) you use. I prefer an ivory or warmer beige to white paper; a better grade of stock is recommended.

● **The Leadership Society Brochure** forms the backbone of your program. You can use it as the basis of a mailing (to introduce Charter Membership in your Societies, for example) or include it by way of explanation with appeals. The focus of the brochure is to remind potential members that they are special.
   The brochure need not be elaborate. A six- or eight-panel format that folds to fit a number ten envelope is easy and effective. You will want to include the following elements:

   ● Cover—announcing/identifying your Societies

- Message from CEO, president or other respected figure thanking donor prospect

- General invitation giving fiscal year parameters, overall information on the purpose of the society

- Specific information on each level of the society

- General information on your organization

● **The Reply Vehicle** can be a two-sided card which fits into a number nine reply envelope. *This is the only reply vehicle you should use. Overrun it for all your solicitations.* The front side of the card sets the tone by proclaiming across the top:
SUPPORT ABC ORGANIZATION AS A MEMBER OF ITS
LEADERSHIP SOCIETIES
The card lists the various categories of Leadership Societies memberships (including Heritage Society) and, of course, indicates that "all gifts, regardless of amount, are warmly appreciated." The reverse side of the card should carry a bequest and planned giving message.

● **Personalized Letters of Appreciation** should be sent along with the reply vehicle as quickly as is possible upon receiving a Leadership Societies gift. Of course, all gifts should be promptly acknowledged (within two weeks of receipt). You should make a special effort to send out your Leadership Societies acknowledgments *within 48 hours.* It helps to have a library of paragraphs or several stock letters to draw upon.

■ **The Enhancements**
Must you offer an incentive premium with a Donor Recognition Program? Of course not! Grassroots organizations and many human services not-for-profits draw heavily from "inner-directed" donors. These individuals are not impressed with physical signs of their participation, although they, even more so than the "outer-directed" donors, appreciate the acknowledgment that they are making a difference.

● **Interest in donor recognition incentives increases with the size of gifts.** I have found that, at the lower levels of donor recognition programs, as few as 20 percent of those who qualify for plaques will ask for them. However, those who do are "outer-directed," and tend to be the most loyal donors.

● **Incentive Premiums come in all sizes, shapes, and prices.** If you decide to offer a premium, whether it is to be a plaque or a pin, a coffee mug or a letter opener, a pen or a piece of original art, the premium represents your organization. The premium you select continues the cultivation process. Will it meet the test of time?

I admit to having a bias toward plaques. They meet my requirements for premiums that have dignity, are highly visible, and cost little. They are also easy to mail.

Typically, I use two types of plaques with my donor recognition programs;

For donors below my major gift level (whether $1,000 or $10,000), I use a format which can be updated for each year of continuing participation with a tab showing the year of the annual gift. This reinforces the habit of annual giving.

A good-looking, yet inexpensive, choice is a parchment certificate which is protected under plexiglass. The certificate can be calligraphed with the name of the donor for personalization. The certificate and plexiglass is mounted on a larger, wood (or wood-simulated) background. The tabs can be placed around the certificate.

For major-gift level donors a larger-sized plaque which uses an etching or illustration in copper, surrounded by a wood background, is always attractive. The donor's name and starting year of membership is personalized on the plaque.

For members of the Heritage (Bequest) Society, you can provide an emblem which can be affixed to the plaques or stand alone, or you may consider a pin.

■ **The acknowledgement vehicle** does not take the place of your personalized letter of appreciation. Rather, it handles three jobs: informing/reminding donors they are members, confirming they will receive a donor recognition incentive, and giving advance notice of the honor roll listing. It is enclosed *with* your letter of appreciation (written on Leadership Society letterhead, of course).

● **Most importantly, the acknowledgement vehicle alerts your donors that they have qualified for your Leadership Society.** Strange as it may seem—with all the emphasis your organization will be putting on educating donors to give at the one hundred dollar and greater level—the majority of your contributors will not consciously register their membership in your Leadership Society unless you bring it to their attention.

● **And you want to emphasize their membership because it helps to create donor loyalty to your organization.** Remember, the more your donor views your organization as his/her charitable priority the less likely you are to be "bumped" when a new, sexier cause comes along.

● **In addition, the acknowledgement vehicle informs donors you intend to publish their names in your annual honor roll.** This advance notice allows them, if they so choose, to request anonymity. This protects you somewhat from accusations that you have not been sensitive to privacy concerns. It also allows you to begin preparing your honor roll early in the year and to learn how donors wish to be listed (Dr. and Mrs. Tom Smith, Mr. Tom and Dr. Mary Smith, Mary and Tom Smith, Mary Smith and Tom Smith, etc.)

● **The acknowledgement vehicle also provides you with the opportunity to let people know whether a plaque or other incentive is being sent automatically or if they must request one.** I recommend automatically providing the incentive for all donors who give over $500. This gives your organization an opportunity for visiting (within logical distances) with your best donors. For those giving $100 to $499, provide the opportunity to request the premium.

● **Finally, your acknowledgement vehicle should let donors know it takes time (four to six weeks is a safe window) to get**

incentives back to them. And, it should give them a name and phone number to contact with questions.

BASIC STRATEGY TO PROMOTE A DONOR RECOGNITION PROGRAM

Your goal, put simply, is to educate as many current and potential donors as possible to accept that a gift of one hundred dollars makes a difference. And to demonstrate to your donors, over and over again, that your organization takes such commitments seriously.

■ **Use all your existing communication vehicles to promote your Leadership Societies.** Include information in every newsletter, any program brochures, and all outreach vehicles. Use the Leadership Society acceptance card as your *only* reply vehicle. The Annual Report with its Honor Roll of Contributors is the showcase for the Leadership Societies. Be sure to use type, print, and copy which sets it off from the rest.

■ **Develop annual giving appeals around the Leadership Society concept.** Chapter 11 on "Soliciting the Annual Gift" provides suggestions.

■ **Be on the lookout for opportunities to share special moments with Society members.** Personalized invitations to the annual meeting, advance announcements of popular events, the chance to meet with visiting dignitaries or share some time with popular members of the staff: communicate with your Society members several times during the year without making the focus of your message a fund raising appeal.

A well-thought-out donor recognition society strengthens your annual giving program and helps to identify appropriate prospects for major, special, and bequest giving. As you read through the next chapters on these fund raising programs, you will find numerous examples of how to incorporate your Leadership Societies into these strategies.

CHAPTER ELEVEN

Creating a "Wish List"

WHY A WISH LIST?

You and I know that your not-for-profit truly benefits the community. Unfortunately, your staff and volunteers are often "tongue-tied" when it comes to giving specific examples of the fine work you do. Too often, you assume others know and understand what is being accomplished and your appeals reflect this vague "doing good" stance. The Wish List gets down to cases and trains your staff and volunteers to articulate what your organization is all about.

The Wish List is more than a brochure. It is a training event as well. It helps to explain the linkage (dare I say the "synergy") between the greater program/service goal and the tangible equipment, staffing, or supplies that support that objective. It works from the bottom up to gather from each and every program area examples that highlight all programs and projects at price ranges, both modest and munificent. Small and simple needs with "price tags" of under $50 as well as major gift opportunities including scholarships, building renovation, facilities namings, and endowment funding costing several thousand or million dollars are included in the final document.

Here are some examples from a Wish List I prepared for the Oregon Trail Chapter of the American Red Cross:

- **Any amount—BLOOD SERVICES**—can be contributed to the Charles Drew Scholarship Fund to train minority students entering the blood banking field.

- **$5.00—BLOOD SERVICES**—tests one unit of blood for all transmissible diseases.

- **$25.00—DISASTER SERVICES**—buys 208 Family Preparedness guides distributed at schools, community center meetings, and events such as the Washington Square Emergency Services Fair.

- **$40.00—COMMUNITY OUTREACH**—funds a field trip or four meetings for teen girls involved with PATHWAYS, a youth diversionary program.

- **$150.00—BLOOD SERVICES**—pays for the shipping costs of 100 units of red cells to support national relief efforts such as the San Francisco earthquake or the Charleston, SC, recovery from Hurricane Hugo.

- **$650.00 each—SAFETY AND HEALTH**—We need fifty "Chris Clean" manikins to train students in First Aid and CPR and meet new federal standards.

- **$1,000.00—COMMUNITY OUTREACH**—builds classroom storage cabinets to house materials for Youth Education programs including Neat Kids/Safe Kids, Where I'm in Charge, Babysitting, and Basic Aid Training.

■ **Yes, the Wish List is truly synergistic!** Attractive and interesting to read, it will accomplish all of the following:

● **Serve as an educational tool** by explaining by example the fine work your organization does. At the same time, it teaches prospects that yours is a complex organization with varied (and often expensive) needs.

● **Encourage upgraded annual giving** by demonstrating how a slightly larger gift makes a difference. Often, modest amounts can be upgraded when suggested that. . . "$75 purchases crayons and art supplies for a class of fifteen children enrolled in our after- school care program."

● **Create an enthusiasm around major and larger gifts** by showing how recognition is accorded to these special donors. Naming opportunities at a variety of giving levels can be included. The Wish List is also useful in conversations with potential major gift/planned gift donors to identify areas of interest. (A more extensive looseleaf notebook listing major gift opportunities of $1,000 and greater with fuller descriptions and photographs/floorplans can be easily prepared from the material you will have gathered.)

● **Alert you to opportunities for publicity** by getting input from the staff and volunteers. Unique needs will surface. These might be of interest to the media. And, if you get a donor who is willing to be spotlighted, you can use this for further publicity.

● **Introduce the idea of bequest and planned giving** by suggesting that, if the desire is present to make a larger than usual gift, staff can work with the prospect to make it come true.

● **Acknowledge and thank volunteers** by including examples of gifts that expand their fine work. The Wish List should include an invitation to volunteer as well—another fine synergy!

And, the Wish List responds to Americans' increasing receptivity to buying from catalogs and direct mail. A Simmons Market Research Bureau survey reported by the Direct Marketing Association in New York City shows that in 1990, roughly 54.4 percent of Americans shopped by mail, compared to only 24.5 percent in 1983.

■ **To create a Wish List** you must do the following:

● **Choose a coordinator.** This can be yourself, an outside consultant, another staff person or a volunteer. But it must be a person who will keep track of deadlines and encourage enthusiastic "buy-ins" from the various departments.

Either the coordinator or her/his delegate will need to:

- choose a format that is attractive and cost effective

- organize the "dollar" list so you avoid duplication

- create the copy that accompanies the dollar listings.

The copy should include:

- a message from the executive director and board chair

- an introduction to the Wish List concept

- information on each general program and service area

- information on volunteering

- information on donor recognition

- information on bequest and planned giving

- a reply vehicle

In addition, you may wish to highlight some of your examples to underscore their urgency to your organization.

● **Hold a full staff meeting.** The executive director must announce the Wish List concept, signalling her/his full support of the project. At this meeting, the coordinator sets follow-up meetings (typically one hour in length) with each program area. Distribute a timeline with deadlines for receiving copy, etc., and the projected date of completion of the Wish List.

• **Involve as many staff, volunteers, and service users as possible in program area followup meetings.** Help that program area to visualize what it does and how. Ask for stories, quotes, favorite photographs, and examples to illustrate the Wish List. Encourage attendees to think both small and large. You want to identify both budgeted items and "pie in the sky" possibilities.

Your examples should explain what is being accomplished by holding the program and providing the service. If multiples of supplies can package a lower-priced item more attractively, include both the per-unit cost and how many (books, sets of crayons, etc.) are used in a week, month, or year.

Ideally, you will receive several examples from each program area demonstrating needs at each of the following steps:

Under $25
$26–$50
$51–$100
$101–$250
$251–$500
$501–$1,000
$1,001–$10,000
Over $10,000

• **Review materials.** Make sure the executive director, heads of department areas, and any other key individuals have an opportunity to review the needs lists before deciding on your format. You'll need to add in overall items, especially capital and endowment needs which may not surface from individual departments. There may also be some duplication of items which can be repackaged. (Example: three xerox machines needed for program centers in Long View, Olympia, and Woodburn.)

■ **What format should your Wish List take?** The Wish List should have a long shelf life; usually at least one to two years. It should be designed so as to avoid references which will date it.

You can organize the Wish List by program areas or goals if your organization is set up that way. Or, use examples from various areas throughout the copy. Arrange the brochure so that items for purchase range from the inexpensive to the expensive. (Don't move from the expensive to the inexpensive: you want prospects to step up, not down.)

The Wish List should contain numerous illustrations as well as quotations, examples, and vignettes about your organization.

Another synergy to remember: the reply device should indicate that gifts can be made in honor or in memory. Indicate you will send a handsome announcement card to whomever the donor designates.

WISH LIST DESIGN TIPS

The Wish List is nothing more or less than a catalog. You want to motivate the reader to "buy." The first objective must be to get his/her attention.

● **Visual Weight:** A brief one-line headline will have more visual impact than a larger, more informative one.

Visual elements such as photos and headlines on the left page receive attention from a good 80 to 100 percent of viewers; the right side's range is a poor 20 to 60 percent.

The best spot on a (two-page spread) is the upper left hand corner of the left page.

The worst spot on a (two-page spread) is the lower right corner of the right page.

● **Initial Point of Focus:** This is the first point on the page that is given attention. The "scan-path," or path of the eye across a page, depends on where the eye starts. if the eye begins on the right page, the left will receive less attention than if the eye started on the left page and moved to the right.

Ideally, initial point of focus is the upper left-hand page.

● **Geometry and Alignment:** A reader will have a much easier time absorbing an orderly page.

Arrange photos and accompanying headlines in a symmetrical pattern.

● **The Visual Hierarchy:** Organize all visual elements on a page in order of priority.

Headlines and photos are, typically, most important and should be arranged to be read/seen first.

Too many visual elements present problems. Don't crowd your layout. The eye stops on 12 to 17 visual elements.

● **Separation:** Photos and headlines should be sufficiently separated so that they are perceived as discrete visual elements.

Use white space or place copy between feature photos.

Source: L. Bruce Hill, Ph.D., Lawson Hill Catalog Marketing, Intervale, NH.

■ **Try to distribute the Wish List as widely as possible.** In addition to your own mailing lists consider offering copies to the public libraries, civic groups and local corporations, etc., to post. If you're fortunate and get initial media coverage, ask the reporter to let readers or viewers know they can request free copies.

■ **Use the Wish List to generate new fund raising strategies.** As you start to group like needs, new ideas for fund raising will surface. You might find logical parallels between some of your needs and various industry and professional groups. For example, your transportation Wish List items might lend themselves to a customer-oriented campaign conducted by the local automotive dealers; the money to solve your food needs could be raised by a Chef's Benefit hosted by the local restaurant association. I've had a professional advertising association raise over $200,000 for a professorship in line with their desire to honor one of their own. Because the group or industry does the fund raising on your behalf it extends your reach.

Having looked fully at the overall synergistic concepts you will use to maximize your development results, let's turn to your potential donors: who are your best prospects?

PART IV

FOCUSING ON YOUR BEST PROSPECTS

With 90 percent of charitable dollars coming from individuals, you need to concentrate your fund raising strategy on gift giving from these folks—not the corporations and foundations. Part four of *Targeted Fund Raising* concentrates heavily on the development strategies that focus on encouraging these prospects to increase current and deferred giving.

Chapter 12 defines the logical prospect universe. Do you know who your best prospects are likely to be? We'll introduce a rule of thumb for how to divide your time and efforts among donors, prospects, and suspects.

Chapters 13 and 14 focus on the area of greatest current potential: individual major donors. First, we'll discuss, in depth, the expanding universe of potential major donors; then, we'll look at how to move your major donor program along.

Finally, chapters 15 and 16 will explore individual fund raising strategies for annual and planned giving.

The 70/20/10 Percent Rule

ONCE HAVING SAID that you should concentrate your efforts on *individuals* who give ninety percent of the philanthropic dollars, rather than foundations and corporations who together give just 10 percent, your best fund raising prospects are those who:

- are already involved with your organization

- are reachable

- have money to give

Makes sense, doesn't it? Yet many not-for-profits don't concentrate their prospecting efforts on individuals who meet these criteria!

YOUR BEST PROSPECTS AND DONORS ARE ALREADY "IN THE FAMILY"

Throw a stone in the water. Look at the ripple. Where is it strongest? *At the center.*

Now, think of your fund raising programs. Where are you spending most of your time and effort?

If you don't answer "at the center" you're doing it backwards.

Savvy fund raisers will spend the majority of the development

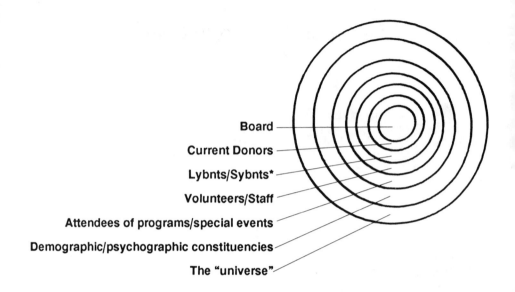

Board
Current Donors
Lybnts/Sybnts*
Volunteers/Staff
Attendees of programs/special events
Demographic/psychographic constituencies
The "universe"

*Donors from "Last year but not this year" and "Some year but not this year"

efforts on renewing and upgrading those who have already made commitments to your organization.

THE 70/20/10 PERCENT RULE OF THUMB

■ **Approximately 70 percent of the fund raising efforts should be positioned at cultivating and soliciting, renewing and upgrading those individuals who already have strong ties to your organization.** Your very best prospects are:

- Members of the Board and Development Committee

- Members of the Staff

- Current Donors

- Current Volunteers

- Current Members

- Retired Board Members

- Retired Staff

- Past Donors (especially LYBNTs—last year but not this year)

- Past Volunteers

- Alumni and Past Members

As much as possible, seasoned development officers use their most personalized fund raising methodologies to reach these individuals. Obviously, you'll need to make choices if you have a large number of prospects to choose from. But, as described in chapter 9: "Synergistic Fund Raising," the goal is to create a smooth transition from your best prospect(s) to your next best to those further down the line.

■ **Approximately 20 percent of the fund raising effort should focus on those who are already familiar with your organization, though not as strongly involved, as the top tier.** This grouping includes:

- Those who have attended one or more of your programs or events

- Those who are clients or have purchased services and/or products affiliated with your organization

- Those who are "related" (parents, grandparents, other family members or close friends) to your closest prospects

Often this group is ready to give but hasn't been made to feel it is "family." You may find using a combination of direct mail and phone calls or a more personalized form of direct mail alone (both are described in chapter 15, "Expanding Your

Results from Annual Giving'') can move significant numbers of this middle ring towards the center.

■ **Only 10 percent of the fund raising effort should be directed at prospects outside of your universe.** This is the most expensive (cost to income ratio) form of fund raising because it is pure acquisition. However, it is essential to keep your universe growing and healthy. The goal is to choose a logical outreach audience. Your efforts are positioned at getting a first gift, regardless of the amount. Your aim is to bring a new individual into your universe.

● **Testing, rather than research, makes sense for trying to identity broad groupings of first-time donors.** Because your goal is first-time involvement at any dollar level, you should try to keep your costs low. Here are some techniques to try:

Find a similar not-for-profit. Identify another not-for-profit—similar in goals and interests to yours—and arrange to swap lists of distant-past or non-donors. A performing arts organization might offer to trade with a fine arts organization its list of one-time ticket buyers for the names of individuals who attended an exhibit but never became members. Neither organization is giving up its best prospects but both gain new potential audiences.

● **Target demographically.** You want to choose those whose demographics or psychographics closely match your current or desired supporters' profiles.

There are several logical groupings of individuals you might consider approaching. Among them are:

- Baby Boomers

- Baby Busters

- Older Individuals

- Hispanic Americans

- Working Women

DEMOGRAPHIC
MARKETING KEYS

TARGETING BABY BOOMERS

- Are just reaching economic maturity

- Not donor/customer loyal

- Grew up being told they were special yet over-whelmed by their own numbers

- Concerned about accountability

- Like straight talk and honest emotion

- Use special events for networking

- Very nostalgic for pre-mid 1960s

- Concentrate on recognition

- Allow time for decision-making

- Key concerns: retirement, college for kids, aging parents

- Focus on instant gratification

TARGETING BABY BUSTERS

- Only 32 million individuals born between 1946 and 1964

- Eventually will be well-positioned economically

- Currently, have high disposable income (parents still paying for much of costs)

- Psychographically, grew up in shadow of the "Boomers"
  —cautious
  —conformist
  —anti-intellectual and pessimistic
  —often fearful, frustrated, and angry

- Favorable toward big business

- Concerns about "quality of life"
  —environment
  —parenting
  —positive self-issues
  —ongoing education

- Reach them now
  —through their parents
  —through the college campus
  —through radio

TARGETING OLDER AMERICANS

- Segment
  —Age 50–64: In transition, young retirees
  —Age 65–74: Traditional givers, smaller numbers
  —Age 75 + : Concerns about outliving assets

- Work niches of concern
  1) the home, 2) health care, 3) leisure, 4) personal and business counselling, 5) education, 6) financial products and services, 7) combating aging

- Avoid negative myths

- Market positively
  —Communicate in length/depth
  —Use appropriate age models, signage, type size
  —Offer new adventures
  —Don't forget about possible new romance

TARGETING HISPANIC AMERICANS

- Be inclusive, not exclusive

- Tend to speak Spanish

- 80 to 90 percent are Roman Catholic

- Are extremely loyal

- Are outer-directed

- Are very family oriented

- Put great emphasis on the importance of education

- The family and community come first

- Major purchasing decisions tend to be made by the man

- Respond to brighter colors, bolder graphics

- Strong users of coupons

TARGETING WORKING WOMEN

- Greatest societal change of the 20th century

- Has shifted attitudes: women feel "ownership" of their money

- Has shifted needs: women are not marrying, need to take control of their finances, planning for retirement

- Uses women's organizations/magazines/etc. for networking

- Aim some prospecting strategies just to women

- Be sensitive about proper recognition

- Be patient

- Accept that many women shy away from recognition

- Concentrate on the goal, not the vehicle

- Understand differences between working women by age/desire to work

For example, for many organizations, women are a logical external audience to cultivate—especially single, working women in their mid-forties or older. They are more charitably inclined than the general population. Many have a strong interest in health, human benefit, and environmental issues. A like-oriented not-for-profit might arrange to buy a list with these demographics.*

Or, you might decide to focus on mature Americans. They account for a substantial and growing percentage—roughly half—of all dollars contributed to charitable causes with those 45–64 representing the most generous donors of all.

---

*A full discussion on fund raising to each of the demographic target groups can be found in my previous books, Changing Demographics: Fund Raising in the 1990s and By the Numbers: Using Demographics and Psychographics for Business Growth in the '90s.

It's fairly simply to rent lists: buy ones targeted to specific demographics. You can even purchase a list of donors to a not-for-profit with similar characteristics to your own organization.

● **Don't immediately send out fund raising appeals to names you acquire.** First, build a sense of belonging. Communication vehicles that stress general imagebuilding, membership, and program opportunities, and invite volunteer involvement will encourage interested individuals and organizations to self-identify. Only then should you send out a solicitation.

Unfortunately, most organizations don't take the time to build a relationship with newly-acquired prospects. The result? Prospects either become low-level donors or never give at all.

■ **My donor and prospect list is small...does the 70/20/10 percent rule still hold?** More so than ever! You'll be gratified at how easily you can surpass your current fund raising benchmark if you continuously focus the bulk of your program on those who are already sold on your organization.

CHAPTER THIRTEEN

The Affluence Explosion: The Real Affluents, The Real Impact

THE IMPORTANCE OF targeting those with the means to give is unprecedented and growing. Unfortunately, a fairly small number of individuals are being targeted by a very large number of not-for-profits. There are just a few truly wealthy individuals in any state and, it often appears that—in violation of the 70/20/10 percent rule of thumb—every not-for-profit considers these to be logical prospects for their organization's fund raising!

Forbes magazine, along with other business and popular publications, loves to tell us who's got the most. In 1990, the annual Billionaires issue trumpeted that there were 99 Americans who made the list with 40 Japanese, 38 Germans, 15 Chinese, and 79 "others" qualifying with net worths over one billion dollars.

Where do the richest Americans live? According to *Forbes*, which annually compiles a list of the 400 richest Americans, New York is home to 105 of America's richest citizens, followed by California, with 62. Several states—Montana, Wyoming, North Dakota, Iowa, Mississippi, Alabama, Georgia, Kentucky, North Carolina, West Virginia, and Maine—have none living within their boundaries. Five of the 400

A heartfelt thanks to Eric Miller, editor of *Research Alert*, who contributed significant portions of this chapter and graciously allowed me to rework it for *Targeted Fund Raising*.

choose to live in other countries: two in England,
two in Switzerland and one in Canada.

**If you can't identify a logical reason for interest, you
don't have a prospect.**

> Many years ago I worked for a small medical college
> specializing in foot disease and disorders. The presi-
> dent and I were trying to identify new prospects for
> the completion of our capital campaign. One day, he
> raced into my office, beaming, and suggested we con-
> tact George Steinbrenner, then owner of the New York
> Yankees. They had met, casually, at a party. I was de-
> lighted, knowing Mr. Steinbrenner met two of our
> major criteria: ability to give and—now—
> accessibility.
>
> But, before setting up an appointment, we
> needed to answer the key question: was it likely Mr.
> Steinbrenner would be interested in helping our
> school? Did he have a relative or friend who was a
> podiatrist? Had he (or a family member or friend)
> benefited from our services? Did ballplayers (gener-
> ally) have bad feet? Unfortunately, research showed
> that all the answers were "no." We decided, regret-
> fully, that Mr. Steinbrenner was not a logical pros-
> pect for our institution.

**However, there are an increasing number of individuals
who can give meaningful gifts, especially if we take cumulative as well as annual giving into account.** The good news is
that, in the past decade, affluence in the United States has increased at a phenomenal rate, enlarging an already essential
market of potential donors.

Using a $60,000 + annual household income as a bench-
mark for affluence, since 1984 the number of affluents have
doubled—and these are low-inflation years, so the increase in
numbers is genuine. For 1990 the total number of affluents in
this country has risen to 37,000,000; that's 9 million more
than in 1985 (a 32 percent increase in five years)—and all indi-
cations are that their ranks will continue to grow. In addition,

there are about 1.5 million households with a net worth of over $1 million.

HOUSEHOLD INCOME DISTRIBUTION
1989 and projected 1994

	1989	1994
0–$9,999	9.8%	7.0%
$10,000–$14,999	5.9%	5.2%
$15,999–$24,999	13.7%	10.3%
$25,000–$34,999	13.5%	10.7%
$35,000–$49,999	18.2%	15.3%
$50,000–$74,999	19.6%	19.9%
$75,000–$99,999	9.3%	14.0%
$100,000–$149,999	7.1%	10.8%
$150,000–$1,999,999	1.7%	4.3%
$200,000 +	1.2%	2.4%

Source: The Affluence Report, Donnelly Marketing Information Service

However, the greater number of affluents in the country has also increased the difficulty of locating them, of separating the truly affluent from those who wear the title by virtue of income but who lack the ways and means of affluence. A combination of finding the real affluents, understanding their values and needs, analyzing their past giving behavior, and knowing how and where to reach them will be the formula for capturing their philanthropic dollars.

WHO ARE THE AFFLUENT?

Defining the affluent market. According to *The Affluent Market Research Program* by Payment Systems Inc., the affluent market—households with incomes of $60,000 or more, or a net worth (excluding the home) in excess of $250,000—has eight distinct subsegments:

- Low End Affluent (41.6%): household head 35 or younger, not retired, 0–1 child and household income of $60–74,999, or more than one child and household income of $75-$99,999, or net worth of $250–$999,999 and income under $50,000;

- High Income, Full Nest (11.3%): household head over 35, not retired, more than one child and household income $60–$74,999;

- Young Affluent (11.4%): household head under 35, household income $60,000 or more, net worth under $1 million, not a senior corporate executive or business owner;

- Career Affluent (10.3%): household head 35 or older, not retired, 0–1 child and household income of $100,000 + and net worth less than $1 million, not a senior corporate executive or business owner;

- Retired Affluent (14.8%): household head retired, household income of $50,000 + or net worth over $250,000;

- Senior Corporate Executive (1.1%): not retired, self-defined corporate executive, income of $100,000 + , net worth between $250,000 and $5 million;

- Business Owner (3.0%): not retired, business owner (half of household income from business), household income of $75,000 + , net worth over $250,000.

In "The Affluence Explosion," a special report from *Research Alert* and *Affluent Markets Alert*, other Niches of Riches are suggested. They include:

- The Mature Market: more than one-third of all U.S. adults, they control half of America's discretionary income and 77 percent of its assets.

- The Gay Market: a seriously neglected and very wealthy segment, the Simmons Gay Media Survey verifies that the gay consumer has a very high income level, a very high educational level, usually no dependents, and, consequently, very high discretionary income.

- The Asian-American Market: with higher educational attainment and a greater number of workers per family, Impact Resources, in profiling consumers with incomes of $75,000 by ethnic background (U.S. index = 100) finds Asians have an index rating of 131, and East Indians have an index of 200 compared to blacks at 55, Hispanics at 47 and whites at 107.

- Middle-Class Millionaires: Donald Trump notwithstanding, often the *appearance* of wealth is in a direct negative relationship with an *accumulation* of wealth. The "typical" millionaire (according to Dr. Thomas J. Stanley, in his book *Marketing to the Affluent*), is a white male business-owner, 57 years old, with two kids, who works 10–14 hours a day, six days a week. There are just over a million and a half millionaires today.

- Childless Households: One-income no-kids households (OINKS) are concentrated in the $100,000 + income range and tend to be older, married, with college backgrounds. Because having a single child eats up 30 percent of the household budget, look to affluent households without kids for big discretionary budgets.

AFFLUENT PSYCHOGRAPHICS

Once we've defined affluence demographically, we need to ask if there are some attitudes, values, and lifestyles—psychographics—affluents have in common. According to a Louis Harris study of 500 households with a minimum of either $100,000 in income or a net worth of $500,000 excluding the value of the primary resident, they do. *Success in America: The CIGNA Study of the Upper-Affluent* notes the following:

- Upper-affluent Americans aren't all "Yuppies." Most are solid, middle-age citizens, with family values and often with grown children.

- The Work Ethic is alive and well in upper-affluent America. They see themselves as hardworking, self-made successes who thrive on giving of themselves; the more successful they are, the less they want to retire.

- The Upper-Affluent are optimistic. They believe their own economic situations will continue to improve or, at worst, hold steady.

- The goals and aspirations of the Upper-Affluent reflect solid values, not a desire for prestige.

- The Upper-Affluent see themselves in control of their financial affairs.

- Real estate, stocks, and money market funds lead investments for the Upper-Affluent.

The real-affluents are those with an affluent mindstyle. Those whose minds lead them to the values, lifestyles, and spending patterns of true affluence. You need to bypass those who fall into some demographic and other research groupings but are not likely to display the psychographic characteristics that make them good prospects for philanthropy.

AFFLUENT GIVING

On the face of it, affluent charitable contributions are impressive. Independent Sector estimates that 94 percent of affluents gave donations in the past year, and the average amount was $1,010, over one-and-a-half times the $640 given by those in the household income group just below them ($35,000–49,999). *However, the percentage of income donated was the lowest of all income groups, 1.4 percent.*

Average 1989 Contribution

Income	Contribution	As a percent of income
Under $10,000	$379	5.5%
$10–$19,999	$485	3.2%
$20–$29,999	$728	2.9%
$30–$39,999	$894	2.6%
$40–$49,999	$831	1.8%
$50–$74,999	$1096	1.8%
$75–$99,999	$2793	3.2%
$100,000 +	$2893	2.9%

Source: Giving and Volunteering in the U.S., 1990, *Independent Sector*

The flip side of this argument is that though wealthy households give smaller percentages of their income to charity than do others, in dollar amounts, their generosity is greater. And, because greater numbers of affluents give, the percentage disparity virtually disappears.

■ **It's been said that the 1990s will be a gentler decade than the 1980s.** Aging baby boomers—key groups of the new affluents—have shifted their focus from acquisition of the necessities of life to concerns for the quality of life around them.

● **Affluents will indeed give more to charitable causes in this decade.** However, the increase will result more from the natural transition of the baby boomers' aging into the always-more-socially-minded middle years than from a new national sense of community.

● **Within 1990s wealth, we long not for lavish parties, spiffy clothes, or speedy cars, but rather for security, freedom, and the financial latitude to be generous.** "Not worrying in the event of illness or emergency" is the number-one reason Americans would like to be rich (according to 81 percent replying to a Gallup Poll). But the desire to be financially able to contribute to others holds up well (63 percent as compared to 55 percent wanting to pass money to children and 46 percent wanting to stop working).

● **The majority of affluent contributions do not go to share-the-wealth causes.** Over half of the dollars given by affluents to philanthropic causes go to institutions that serve their interests and values—private education, medical institutions, and cultural organizations. Affluents are not altogether altruistic with the points of light they wish to offer back to the society that has served them. Independent Sector reports that affluents are the most likely of income groups to blame the new tax laws for cutting back on charitable donations (13 percent), even though they are the group most likely to still qualify for full deductions for charities, i.e., high-income itemizers. Affluents keep their hands out of their pockets when confronted with street beggars. Affluents are more likely to see homeless people than other income groups, are approached the most frequently for handouts, and give more rarely than others.

MARKETING TO AFFLUENTS

A key to the giving of this decade will be that the donations of the real-affluents will actually be "buying" experiences and feelings that they value.

■ **The affluent market in the 1990s is one of stabilization.** The affluent sector will be very concerned with the preservation of its money and lifestyle. Households that joined the ranks of the affluent in the last decade will be doing everything they can to keep from getting squeezed back down to the middle. Affluents are feeling the pinch of a weak economy and tight money.

■ **What's important to the 1990s affluent is value.** Affluent consumers value "value" itself. Affluents value the perceived quality of a product or service, as well as which products and services they think of as "high end" or "quality" offerings.

The motivating forces behind new ideas of value are evident in some basic shifts in the more traditional sense of the word "values." Families are "in"; affluents have larger households than average. Affluents seek ways to make up for the time they spend in busy careers by seeking goods and services that sell the hottest affluent commodity of the nineties: time. And, there is more concern for the rest of the world—expressed in affluents' stated concerns about the ills of society and of the environment (as well as what factors they consider as they make their purchases and their charitable donations).

Say "quality" and "novelty" to the affluent, and mean it, and you'll get their attention. But keep in mind that while experimentation is important, those affluents who are time-pressed will stick to what they know really works, getting the most value for their money and time. While affluents like novelty, they also demand significant information before purchasing. In the end, a brand name that says quality will win out over novelty.

■ **What qualities do affluents value?** According to *Town & Country* magazine:

- disdain for the mediocre

- education

- elevated levels of taste

- "good name"—honesty

- character, integrity.

Add to this, pragmatism. Affluents look for what works. They are less "big government" in their view, but want the homeless housed and the environment improved, and they want the federal government to do it. They are fairly liberal on many social issues—abortion and homosexuality, for example—but are fairly conservative on economic issues.

They often ask for more information and less hype in advertising; they feel they can decide based on the facts. To sell them anything, convince them that it works, that it makes sense. Bear in mind that they are savvy enough with advertising to spot hype a mile away, and to be skeptical of claims. "Skeptical" is perhaps the most apt word for their attitude— they've heard it all before; yet, they are not cynical. One of the luxuries of affluents is the belief that goodness is predominant, and that they can make things work out.

■ **How do you address affluents effectively?** The Roper Organization offers some general rules-of-thumb to keep in tune with affluent lifestyles and mindstyles. All of these guidelines draw from (as well as support) the variety of data about affluents: they address the mindstyle of affluence, with respect to the affluents' somewhat sensitive reactions to high-pitched pleas. They address the special characteristics of the affluents (and increased appetite for information) that translate into an affluent predilection for articles (instead of ads that are long on hyperbole and short on information).

Rules for Reaching Affluents

- Articles—as opposed to advertisements—are more effective for reaching Affluents. They trust the printed word more than do other consumers. Also, they spend more time reading.

- Use specialty magazines and journals.

- Using radio and television? Pay attention to programming: public affairs and sports programs are good.

- Direct response campaigns—minus any hard sell—have strong appeal.

- Affluents spread the word among other affluents.

- Affluents often chose the quickest way to communicate: the telephone.

- They trust instant buying and aren't squeamish about giving their credit card numbers over the phone.

Messages should:

- emphasize discovery and exploration, not the known;

- appeal to knowledge and judgment, not status;

- be a challenge, not a guarantee;

- show action, not passivity;

- provide news, not hype;

- project decisiveness, not hesitancy;

- reveal a broad-minded sense of cooperation and independence, rather than competition.

To wrap up, market philanthropic giving as if it were a product. Affluents demand quality and want to see a return—

Source: *The Influential Americans: Who They Are, How to Reach Them,* The Roper Organization

experiential or otherwise—on their investment. As any product marketer does, a philanthropic marketer should make ex-
plicit the benefits of buying his product, i.e., making a
donation. Affluents are well informed, educated people; they
want to know that their donation is going to make a solid, con-
crete difference. Show how the organization will use their gift.
Provide them with a breakdown of everything their donation
will make possible. Pragmatism and quality are the attributes
that affluents desire in their purchases; make sure they are
aware that their giving will produce a definite result.

CHAPTER FOURTEEN

Targeting Major Donor Dollars

IT WOULD BE WONDERFUL if everyone you identified as a prospect for fund raising could be cultivated and solicited face-to-face. That's the most effective form of fund raising.

But, for most organizations, that's simply not realistic. Given a wealth (no pun intended) of current donors and logical prospects, we need to make hard choices about who is a priority and who is not. That determines who will be handled more personally and who receives only direct mail.

If you follow the 70/20/10 percent rule, you'll know where to start. The majority of your major gifts prospects—those you'll handle face-to-face—are individuals within the closest rings of your family. Concentrate your research efforts on:

- Members of the Board and Development Committee

- Members of the Staff

- Current Donors

- Current Volunteers

- Current Members

- Retired Board Members

- Retired Staff

- Past Donors (especially LYBNTS—last year but not this year)

- Past Volunteers

- Alumni and Past Members

When you've gone through those lists—using the input of your development committee, board and staff as well as the public data bases and your local media—you may not need, initially, to go any further to identify your first top 25. But, if you do, choose additional prospects from:

- Those who attend your programs or special events

- Those who buy products or services affiliated with your organization

- Those who are "related" (parents, grandparents, other family members or close friends) to your closest supporters

Once you've decided who your best prospects are, you need to keep their names constantly in the forefront of your board and staff's attention.

The problem is that, too often, even the most seasoned development director gets overwhelmed by the possibilities and nothing moves along. To narrow down the potential into action steps becomes a priority. Whether you use a sophisticated, computerized tracking system or rely on handwritten notes, you must develop "at a glance" summary sheets that you can use easily and are comfortable sharing with others.

Building a "Top 25" Prospect List

■ **Start building a "Top 25" prospect list for individuals.** Rank prospects according to your assessment as to their accessibility and likelihood of gift giving. The lists provide a quick visual reminder of who's moving along and who's not.

Redo the lists each month for the immediate three-month period. Using accounting paper, or columns, provide the following pieces of information for each prospect:

- What is the connection?

- What is the likely range of the gift?

- What is the likely project/program to be funded?

- Who is to serve as the contact?

- What is your strategy? The next step? Timing?

ABC ORGANIZATION
Major Giving Prospects, July 199-

Name	Connection/$Potential/Interest	Contact Person	Strategy Step
A	Mrs. A's mother, memorial naming of library, $250,000	Sue L.	visit 7/18
B	New board member, scholarship endowment, $1,000,000	Jack R.	lunch with CEO 9/2
C	Alumnae, retirement concerns possible unitrust, $500,000	Bill D.	call 7/15
D	Unsolicited giver of $10,000 learn area of interest	Donna W.	visit 8/20
E	No current affiliation with us. Gives to similar organizations $20,000 +	Bob T.	visit/tour facility 8/1

The sample list demonstrates several important facts quickly:

- It tells the board and staff who needs to be moved along during the next three months and what steps are to be taken.

- It tells the board and staff who has the responsibility for taking those steps.

- It identifies those prospects for whom more information is needed and alerts board and staff to look for connections.

● **Why limit it to 25?** For most organizations, the director of development must closely orchestrate prospect identification, cultivation and solicitation or it doesn't happen. I have found that three lists of twenty-five or less (one each for individuals, corporations, and foundations) is the most you can track easily if your goal is results.

■ **When you begin your lists you may think you have fewer than twenty-five prospects.** That's not true unless the total number of your prospects is under twenty five! You've simply fallen into the trap of assuming your top prospects must give at a particular level. *Regardless of whether your top prospect can give $2,500,000 or $2,500 or $25, you cannot afford not to upgrade and move that prospect along!*

Of course, it's possible that none of your top prospects can, in fact, give large enough gifts to handle the goals of your organization. If so, you've identified a strong need to bring some additional prospects into your family—the 10 percent rule of thumb.

That need is shown on our chart with the inclusion of "Ms/Mr E"—who supports organizations similar to ABC at a major level. Luckily for our illustrating organization, ABC's board member (Bob T.) knows "Ms/Mr E" and is able and willing to open the door.

■ **You may be overwhelmed with possibilities and have trouble prioritizing.** Lucky you! But, unless you've got an unusually large number of active board members and staff to follow up on prospects, resist the temptation to put everyone on your list. As you move your top prospects along from cultivation to solicitation to gift-giving some will (temporarily) move off your top 25 list. This gives you the chance to move others on. Eventually you may need to attach a secondary summary sheet detailing the names of others just below the top 25.

CULTIVATING AND SOLICITING YOUR "TOP 25"

Once you've put together a list of individuals capable of making larger gifts, you need to understand the "triggers" that can move prospects along. The relationship between the fund raiser and the major gifts prospect cannot be adversarial. In seeking to match up a potential donor with a project or program that addresses his/her area of concern, we look for "win-win" situations. In a sense, once the prospect expresses interest, the development officer must sit on the "same side of the table," working as much for the prospect as for the organization the fund raiser represents.

This "voluntary exchange of benefits," cited by Philip Kotler in *Marketing for Nonprofit Organizations* is marketing. No matter how worthy, your organization's needs and goals will not call forth support from the private sector unless the needs and goals of the potential donor are equally met.

Not-for-profits have become increasingly sophisticated at articulating missions, goals, and objectives in ways that facilitate this exchange. Using psychographics, the fund raiser can pinpoint the values, attitudes, and lifestyle particulars that will determine the general type of program/project the potential donor is likely to find of interest **and** the best time in the lifecycle of a program/project to involve him/her. This can be the key to quicker decision making on the part of the major gift prospect.*

My previous books, *Changing Demographics: Fund Raising in the 1990s* and *By the Numbers: Using Demographics and Psychographics for Business Growth in the '90s* (Bonus 1990), each devote several chapters to explaining how to use psychographics—values, attitudes, and lifestyles—to structure the major gifts/purchase cultivation and solicitation process more effectively.

CHAPTER FIFTEEN

Expanding Your Results from Annual Giving

MOST ORGANIZATIONS differentiate between the larger number of smaller gifts solicited yearly through the annual gift campaign and a smaller number of larger gifts cultivated through the major donor program. Too often, the annual gift campaign is viewed as a nuisance: taking a great deal of time for very little in results.

This needn't be the case at your organization. As we discussed in previous chapters, large numbers of your current and future prospects are both economically capable and psychologically positioned to make annual gifts of one hundred dollars and greater.

METHODOLOGIES FOR ANNUAL GIVING

If your organization has a very small base of current donors and prospects to cultivate and solicit for annual gifts, set up face-to-face appointments for *all* of them. It is the most effective way to receive meaningful gifts.

But, assuming you have more than a few dozen donors and prospects, this will probably not be possible. Once you have decided on the prospects volunteers and staff will contact personally or in group settings, you'll need to move to the next steps:

Telecommunications and Telemarketing

Limited by your logistics (phone lines available/ callers you have)	1. Larger number can be reached but cost (as a %) is much higher	Combination of Direct Mail (cultivation) and Phone (solicitation)
Limited by your logistics (as in 1)	2. Larger number Poorer fulfill- ment	Phone calls alone

GOAL: Renewal and upgrading. Educating donors to give at the $100 + level of support.

Direct Mail

Limited by your knowledge of base and com- puter capability	3. Larger numbers Poorer fulfill- ment	Personalized
Limited only by budget	4. Largest num- bers. Poorest response	Non- personalized

GOAL: Acquisition of new donors, ideally at the $100 + level of support, but—primarily—to keep the donor base expanding.

Note: A new communications technology, the 900 and 700 telephone options, where the cost of the call is borne by the prospect/donor, has recently become available. This, along with 800 numbers where the organization pays for the telephone calls, may be a viable acquisition methodology for larger not-for-profits to consider.

Again, work through the "breaks" of your fund raising strategy. While a combination of direct mail and phone follow-up can be the most effective strategy for reaching the next level of the prospect pool, you'll need to decide whether you can use this for all of the remainder of your prospects or if you need to step your strategy down to direct mail.

Regardless of which strategy or strategies you decide to employ, the key to annual getting in the 1990s will lie in your ability to make potential donors feel good about giving.

HELPING DONORS TO DETERMINE A MEANINGFUL COMMITMENT LEVEL

■ **Annual-giving face-to-face solicitations provide the opportunity to help prospects focus on how much they care about your organization.** When individuals ask me "how much should I give annually?" my answer is always "at whatever level is a 'meaningful commitment' for you." Then I suggest the following exercise to help determine what a meaningful commitment can be.

● **Pick an activity you enjoy and do regularly for leisure.** Going to the movies, eating out, bowling, skiing are all good choices. Figure out how much you spend each time you do it. Multiply that by the number of times you do it.

● **The money you spend on leisure is disposable income—the same "pocket" we use for charitable giving.** Very few people are saints: we don't expect to give up meals or do without necessities to make contributions. We choose to give either in addition to or instead of activities of choice.

● **Ask yourself "how important is the ABC Organization to me?"** If your answer is "as or more important than going to the movies, eating out, bowling, skiing, etc." you should consider demonstrating that commitment by making a gift equal to or in excess of the amount you are spending on that activity.

■ **You can create a similar climate through a combination of direct mail and telephone communications.** I was once asked to describe the relationship between cultivation and solicitation. I compared it to a wall chart at the American Museum of Natural History in New York City: the history of the earth (cultivation) is a line nearly thirty yards long; the history of man (solicitation) is less than one quarter inch.

● **Too often, we skip the cultivation steps in our annual appeals and move right into the solicitation.** Today's donors and prospects are demanding fuller information about our organizations.

Be sure your appeal letters include the following steps:

An explanation of what is being asked. Tell your prospect immediately that you will be asking for money. Let her/him know you consider her/him to be important to your organization and will be asking for a significant commitment.

Full information on what your organization is and does using specific examples. Make this personal—have your letter signer or caller indicate what the organization means to him/her as well.

A request for a meaningful commitment. Show your prospect how he/she can make a major gift in installments. "Please consider making a quarterly gift of $50 over three years for a total commitment of $600." (More about this in the next section.)

A closing that thanks your prospect and reminds him/her about the Leadership Societies. Emphasize the one hundred dollar giving level in both your final paragraph and in the postscript.

■ **Know why you're asking for a gift.** As we discussed in chapter 6, "Creating a Successful Fund Raising Board," you can't raise money for the development department. Regardless of whether you're targeting a donor who will give one hundred dollars or one million, you must be able to provide clear examples of how the money raised will be used. Your annual donors have just as much interest as your major donors in knowing the programs and projects their dollars will support.

■ **Don't ask for general operating funds.** Your donors are restricting their gifts at lower and lower levels. (To discourage this, you need a policy as part of your gift stewardship guidelines that encourages unrestricted gifts.) You must try to separate out the needs you "lumped' into general support. Do specific appeals. A college, for example, can schedule separate mailings on bookplate namings in the library and/or tribute namings for modest scholarships instead of repeating the annual alumni appeal.

■ **Make your requests for gifts timely.** Tie it to the calendar: the start of the fiscal year ("Starting the year as a member of the Leadership Society"); the end of the calendar year ("An opportunity to help while gathering tax advantages"); and the close of the fiscal year ("Will your name lead the 199- Honor Roll of Donors?").

■ **Use donor recognition to encourage larger annual gift-giving.** The Leadership Societies concept, discussed in detail in Chapter Ten, "Begin by Saying Thank You," should be used to educate donors and prospects about giving at the one hundred dollar level and higher.

● **Announce the formation or reformation of your donor recognition program in a campaign of its own.** "Charter membership" can be a powerful appeal: you can use it to suggest a reason for immediate upgrading before the end of the fiscal year. Or, position a special series of solicitations just before the start of a new fiscal year to current members: thank them for their past support and invite them to set a new standard for the coming year.

**You can increase the results of
your direct mail appeals.**

● The Northeast region is most charitably responsive to direct mail (21%) with Massachusetts the leading state (26%), followed by the New York-New Jersey area (23%). Those in the West and North Central have a 15% response rate; the South 13%. Oklahoma with 5% and Arizona with 7% are least responsive.

- Non-profits and other fund raisers send out more direct mail appeals in November than any other month. The lightest month for direct mail is June.

- Almost 90% of individuals surveyed say brochures play a role in their buying decisions; 25 percent said brochures play a key role.

- Color can increase readership by 41 percent, increase the reader's retention by 18 percent, and can raise a buyer's tendency to purchase by 26 percent.

- A typed envelope usually outpulls a self-mailer. Use reflex blue for signing: it looks more like a signature.

- What makes a great letter? Start with a hook; give the facts fast; end the letter persuasively. Ask for money up front.

● **Use the Leadership Societies as a secondary theme in every appeal you send.** Whether you are asking for funds for scholarship or a piece of equipment, trying to avert a crisis or stretching to meet a challenge, suggest that your prospect *consider making his/her gift as a member of your Leadership Society.* Continuously reinforce prospects' and donors' understanding that it takes a gift of one hundred dollars or greater to create change.

HOW DO YOU ENCOURAGE YOUR DONORS AND PROSPECTS TO MAKE ANNUAL GIFTS AT A HIGHER, MORE FULFILLING LEVEL?

■ **Your "family" cares about your organization. Help them say yes.** There are nineteen ways to say no to a request for a donation. The majority of these have to do with timing, not caring. *Too often we don't help our donors and prospects to find the satisfaction that larger gift-giving provides.*

- **Most donors look at their checkbook balance when deciding on gift amounts.** Few of us would be comfortable writing a large check for charity. Assuming you want to make a gift of $250, it's often difficult to actually put the money aside for one payment. Instead we choose an amount, typically $25 or $10, because these small contributions don't upset our budgets. But, if we made that same gift of $25 or $10 *month after month*, our small but steady contributions would result in significant dollars. Your strategy must be to encourage donors to pick "the check commitment level" they are comfortable with and write that check over and over again—weekly, monthly, quarterly.

- **Focus on a high total gift amount over time.** "Please consider making a quarterly gift of $50 over three years for a total commitment of $600." The total amount of the request—$600—tells the prospect you think s/he is important to your organization. Most donors would prefer to be significant. The check commitment level—$50—suggests an upgrade from prior gifts of $25. Giving quarterly shows the prospect how to budget to accomplish the goal.

  Your prospect may not commit to the total $600 requested but will usually pick an annual gift amount well above her/his typical $25.

  To reach the higher dollar amounts in annual giving, you'll have to encourage use of the fund raising vehicle that makes giving less painful: pledging.

■ **Frequent giving increases donor loyalty as well as gift levels.** Not only will you get more money through pledging, you will be more likely to retain your annual donor. Steve Woodworth, vice-president of marketing at World Vision in Monrovia, California, makes four points about monthly givers:

- *Monthly pledging breaks the psychological barrier.* "Donors who would not consider themselves $200 donors will make a commitment to send $20 per month.''

- *It's the ultimate involvement device.* With monthly pledges, ''donors consider themselves more a part of the organization and are less likely to lose interest.''

- *Gift income from monthly pledges is more stable than income from once-a-year gifts* and ''it is more predictable and it is less influenced by the general climate.''

- *If you're using high-cost acquisition vehicles, monthly pledges are sometimes the only way to acquire new donors and show a profit.* A $20 gift ''sells'' more easily than a $240 gift.

TODAY'S ANNUAL DONOR, TOMORROW'S MAJOR OR PLANNED DONOR

Continuously cultivate your annual donors now for the future. Remember the 70/20/10 percent rule: it's from within your ''family'' that tomorrow's major and planned gifts will come. Be sure to make renewal and upgrading your priority. Follow each successful solicitation with a meaningful gesture of appreciation. Keep your circle unbroken.

CHAPTER SIXTEEN

Sowing for a "Harvest" of Bequests and Planned Gifts

ACCUMULATING, SAVING AND managing money will be major preoccupations for most of America in the years ahead. Living longer brings with it concerns about living well. For that reason, many not-for-profits will find that, increasingly, major gifts will *not* be current gifts but rather the combination of current and deferred gifting we call planned giving.

■ **The market for planned giving is expanding along with the number of newly affluent individuals.** As discussed in chapter 13, the affluent—as compared to the truly wealthy—are a significant new market for fund raising. James Keating, president of Endow America, notes that the affluent are especially important prospects for planned giving, capable of creating high "face value" gifts from their large discretionary incomes.

■ **Planned giving is the necessary complement to your annual and major giving programs.** It enables your individual donors to make partially or fully deferred gifts to your organization while receiving immediate recognition and possible tax benefits.

THE MARKETING APPROACH TO PLANNED GIVING

■ **Don't fall into the trap of assuming the number one concern of your prospect is tax advantages.** Research has shown—over and over again—that most donors consider tax breaks as

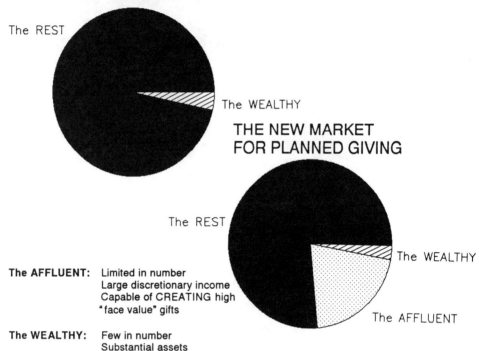

THE OLD MARKET
FOR PLANNED GIVING

The REST

The WEALTHY

THE NEW MARKET
FOR PLANNED GIVING

The REST

The WEALTHY

The AFFLUENT

The AFFLUENT: Limited in number
Large discretionary income
Capable of CREATING high
"face value" gifts

The WEALTHY: Few in number
Substantial assets
Capable of GIVING a major gift

The REST: Large in number
Limited discretionary income
Capable of CREATING low "face value" gifts

"icing," not the primary reason for gift giving. Belief in your
organization, in the work it does, and the people it serves are
the overwhelming reasons why people give.

■ **Baby boomers may be entering a new financial stage of life:
shifting from consumption and the present to savings and the
future.** Joseph McCarthy, president of the New York investment
firm Lord Abbett, firmly believes that baby boomers are about
to start the biggest investment boom ever. McCarthy suggests
that unprecedented inheritances from the parents of boomers
will accentuate the trend, swelling stock market averages as
boomers inherit bonds and stock certificates from their
income-oriented parents and shift them to growth-oriented

stocks. This makes sense when you review Ken Dychtwald's assessment of the boomer's financial style noted in chapter 3.

- **A properly executed bequest and planned giving program gives your donors a bit of immortality.** The majority of adults today are baby boomers, individuals who were brought up by doting parents and a society which taught them to believe they were special. *Psychologically, boomers see themselves as major givers but often lack the immediate resources to make significant current gifts.* Planned giving creates a bridge between their desires and reality.

In spite of—or because of—strong peer economic competition, many boomers live in a world where sophisticated financial planning is a mark of status. *Money, Inc., Entrepreneur*—these magazines owe their success to a heavily boomer audience.

Not-for-profits and insurance companies have teamed up to market to this psychographic trigger. Colleges and universities are now inviting boomers to "make a relatively modest contribution today that matures into a major gift in the future" through a fund raising program that "establishes a trust fund with life insurance as its vehicle."

The positioning is important: a 45-year-old prospect can make a major gift of $50,000 for only $1,740 a year over a five-year period, for a fully tax-deductible total pledge of $8,700.

Boomers like financial vehicles which reinforce their sense of self.

- **Boomers may be receptive at younger ages than other groups to planning for retirement.** According to Jeff Ostroff, author of *Successful Marketing to the 50 + Consumer*, baby boomers—unlike today's 45- to 65-year-olds—are more informed about the need to plan for retirement early. "They'll know, for example, that retirement could last 30 years or more. (They) will be unlikely to rest comfortably at night knowing they can depend on Social Security or Medicare in their later years." Ostroff believes life insurance, private pension vehicles, and conservative savings programs will all do well. *Couple this with a desire to make a difference and you have a key marketing thrust for more than one-half the adult population!*

Retirement is not the only boomer financial concern:

- **Market to their concerns for providing for their children's college educations.** Because boomers married later and had children later, many—when they hit their fifties—will still be struggling with tuition payments. Robert Hewitt, president of the International Association of Financial Planners, believes that, as the first broadly college-educated generation, boomers will want to save more than their parents did for their children's tuition. And they will do more of their savings and investing in mutual funds, rather than in individual stocks, bonds or bank accounts.

   Among parents of children aged three or younger, education is the biggest concern they have for their children's future, according to a survey by Gerber Products Company of Fremont, Michigan. Twenty-six percent of parents are concerned about the quality and cost of providing an education for their children.

   And concerns about financing a college education rise with income, finds the American College Testing Program of Iowa City, Iowa, in a survey sponsored by *Money* magazine. While 28 percent of all family decision-makers worry about college costs, this proportion rises to 45 percent among those with household incomes of $50,000 or more.

   Savvy financial marketers are going to colleges and universities, suggesting partnerships that provide finder's fees to the school while benefiting alumni. The UCLA Alumni Association has become the first such organization to offer a program to assist parents in saving for their children's college education. The CollegeSure CD is especially appealing to mobile boomers because it can be used at any college or university. The concept was developed by Paine Webber, Inc.

- **Market to boomers as a "sandwiched" generation.** Robert Hewitt thinks the big shock to the boomer generation will not be the bills associated with their children, but those associated with their parents. Instead of the inheritances McCarthy envisages, Hewitt points to the long-term health-care costs that could erase those inheritances.

■ **Right now, although they represent only 25 percent of the total U.S. population, Americans over 50 have a combined annual personal income of over $800 billion and control 70 percent of the total net worth of U.S. households—nearly $7 trillion of wealth.** The over-50 group controls 50 percent of the discretionary income in the United States and 77 percent of the financial assets.

The "elderly" (age 65–74) receives 80 percent more income than average from estates, trusts, dividends, and rentals. The value of their assets is almost 21 percent greater than average.

Households headed by people aged 75 and older have income from estates, trusts, dividends, and rentals that is more than twice the average. The "aged" and the "very old" have assets with a value 5 percent above average.

Unlike the younger prime lifer/baby boomer, Jeff Ostroff says the more "senior" market's predominant concern will be the **management** of money. "For this reason, many older adults are likely to need the services of those who can help them oversee their assets, pay their bills, and protect their estates. Need for these services will be buoyed by the growth of the over-75 population, some of whom will be unable to handle these matters themselves but who will have the money to pay for them. Others, similarly unable, will have children willing to pay for the help."

Among the financial products and services likely to be in demand by the senior population and well-positioned for a planned giving program are:

- CDs, savings accounts, money-market mutual funds, and government-backed securities

- Estate planning

- Trust fund/portfolio management

■ **Here are some marketing keys to use with older Americans:**

● **Market positively!** Especially when marketing financial planning to older Americans, we have a tendency to describe negative "what if" scenarios. Today's mature American is more likely to be interested in life income vehicles that enhance a comfortable retirement than a financial planning vehicle which saves inheritance taxes.

● **Recognize they hold conservative attitudes towards money** and select financial institutions with guaranteed-safe investments, a high rate of return, and convenience as their priorities. They want to deal with people—not automatic teller machines. People aged 50 and over tend to keep their money in several institutions rather than consolidating their assets.

● **Help them be more effective consumers** by offering financial seminars free of charge. Ostroff points out that a more educated older population "will thirst for information to help it function well in a rapidly changing marketplace. This will increase the desirability and marketability of those with specialized expertise in the areas of greatest interest to older consumers—particularly health care, financial services, and travel/leisure." (Be sure to schedule your financial planning seminars in the daytime. Many older persons dislike driving at night because of vision problems.)

● **Help them guard the nest.** Often, older Americans have been widowed or divorced and remarried or have a "significant other." Romance at later ages also brings with it concerns for protecting assets. Sensitive financial planning advice may be welcome by the entire family.

● **Don't assume they won't purchase nest-building vehicles.** Regardless of the level of income and assets, mature households' purchases of life insurance, endowments, and annuities are about the same as the national average, suggesting that mature consumers are still building estates.

● **Seek out the "elder" newcomers to your community.** Many of the more affluent mature Americans "migrate" on retirement to cities and towns that provide cultural, educational, and recreational opportunities. College towns, for example, are becoming choice retirement spots. Eugene, Oregon; Madison, Wisconsin; Austin, Texas; Ann Arbor, Michigan; Williamstown, Massachusetts; Ithaca, New York; Burlington, Vermont; Annapolis, Maryland; Charlottesville, Virginia; Hanover, New Hampshire; and Chapel Hill and Winston-Salem, North Carolina, are showing significant growth in their mature populations. Work with realtors, chambers of commerce, and welcome wagons to find such individuals and help them get settled financially.

■ **Are you marketing your planned giving program heavily to women?** You should. After all:

● **Women outlive men.** *Women own 89 percent of the wealth of this country.* Women control the disposition of their own estates and, often, that of the spouse as well.

● **Women are increasingly not marrying** and are taking responsibility for their own retirements and estate planning.

● **Women are becoming more affluent.** The numbers of women earning over $50,000 doubled from 1980 (6 percent) to 1986 (12 percent). As we continue into the twenty-first century the gains will expand.

A survey of its readership by *McCall's* magazine indicates that while, as a group, women are "financially fairly savvy," many have not taken responsibility for handling their own financial resources. "Forty-one percent have never had a bank loan in their own names; 33 percent do not have their own checking accounts; 46 percent do not have savings and investment objectives; 44 percent have never personally made investments in stocks, bonds, mutual funds or real estate; 59 percent have no income-replacement options in the event they become disabled; a shocking 42 percent don't know their entitlements under their own and/or their spouse's Social Security and pensions; and *43 percent are without a financial plan to prepare for retirement*."

■ Younger working women are a largely untapped market of opportunity for planned giving programs. Here are some marketing suggestions to consider:

● **Market to women earlier.** Women are ready for financial advice at earlier and earlier ages. Begin to prospect to women in their mid-forties. Increasing numbers of more affluent women are remaining single or become single at mid-life through divorce or widowhood. These women have greater earning potential in their own right as well as the continued traditional access to wealth from deceased family members. They are greatly concerned about providing for their own retirements and the eventual disposition of their assets. And many are the caregivers to parents and grandparents, handling financial responsibilities for multiple generations.

● **Prospect specifically for affluent women.**

   • Using Standard and Poors, Who's Who in American Women, etc., find prospects within your "family." Set appointments now.

   • Follow up with all referrals of women even if, on the surface, they don't appear to be good prospects. Women have not been cultivated, by and large, and are often overlooked by the largely male financial-planning community.

● **Aim some prospecting strategies specifically at women.** You can't treat a woman just like a man. And many women are extremely sensitive to any perception of being patronized.

Provide women with resources. Hold seminars and workshops on financial planning. Focus a segment on issues of concern for women. Show women in roles as financial advisors. Send a quarterly newsletter which focuses on retirement planning from the female perspective.

Educate your financial advisors to be sensitive. Hold workshops for lawyers and trust officers with special segments on the concerns of the women prospects. Women tend to be more conservative than men, often favoring less risky financial vehicles and looking for demonstrated fiscal accountability.

Write articles for local women's groups to include in their newsletters. Include tax information and bequest information.

Prepare a talk on the subject of women and financial planning and present it at women's service and professional organizations.

Visit women. Try to see all the women on your prospect list. Take a few months and see **only** women. You'll be surprised at how much you've been concentrating on men prospects.

● **Women are your best prospects for using a charitable planned gift** but prefer to honor others through their giving. The opportunity to pay tribute to a parent or other loved one is more likely to trigger a gift than a chance for personal recognition. *And, be patient.* Recognize that many women are more concerned with their ability to replace gifts of wealth. Their first use of a life income vehicle will probably be modest.

■ **More than 90 percent of Hispanics agree that "saving a portion of one's income is the best way to plan for the future" and "it is essential for a man with a family to have life insurance,"** according to the *Hispanic Monitor,* a report by Market Development of San Diego, California, and Yankelovich Clancy Shulman of Westport, Connecticut.

Often minority populations are ignored marketing targets for financial planners. Many Hispanic Americans feel their business is not appreciated. Although it is true that median incomes of minority households are often below those of white households, there are still pockets of opportunity for savvy planned-giving officers.

● **Carve out a niche that welcomes the modest dollar planned-giving prospect.** Because Hispanic-Americans are younger than the full population, most of the key "life events"—marriage and births, for example—lie ahead of them. They are likely prospects for insurance and trusts for children's education.

● **Make your organization welcoming.** Offer materials in both English and Spanish. Have financial planners who are conversant in both languages. Advertise in Hispanic publications.

● **Market, psychographically, to outer-directedness.** Identify role models from the Hispanic community who can provide testimonials as to the value of financial planning. Let your prospects know they have been selected as community leaders and ask them to suggest other prospects.

● **Respond to the sense of family.** Use direct response ads (remember, Hispanic Americans have the highest response rate to coupons) to invite parents to seek information on planning for children's educations. Or to discuss handling financial concerns with aging parents.

● **Cultivate now for the years ahead,** by increasing your organization's visibility with Hispanic constituencies. Offer complimentary financial planning sessions through the churches, fraternal and civic organizations. Become involved with the Hispanic community. Learn who the leaders and influential citizens are and find out what needs you can help with.

WHY MANY ORGANIZATIONS NEGLECT PLANNED GIVING

■ **The results of a bequest and planned giving-program may take three to five years to emerge.** For that reason, too often, the board and the development director put bequest and planned gifts last on their list of priorities. The board worries: we can't count on these gifts. The development director frets: if I do the work but the gift doesn't come in for five, ten, twenty years, should I spend the time?

■ **Many not-for-profits mistakenly believe a planned giving program is beyond their expertise.** For most organizations the emphasis of the program will be on bequests. Leaving a gift by will is simple to understand and not very complicated to do. Even if you and your board have concerns about the more sophisticated forms of planned gifts such as annuities and trusts, pooled income funds, insurance, real estate, securities and other personal property, begin by encouraging gifts by bequest.

> The correct response to both concerns lies in understanding our dual responsibilities:
>
> • to provide donors with all the tools to maximize current gift giving
>
> and
>
> • to build a base of private support that will provide our organizations with financial stability in the future.

And, while you can't easily predict when the dollars will be available, you can track growth and set objectives through the numbers of bequest and planned gift notifications. The goal for your first year of the program might be to receive five bequest notifications; for year two, the goal might be to receive ten bequest notifications and initiate one planned gift.

THREE PARTS TO A PLANNED GIVING PROGRAM

■ **Planned giving requires the development director to handle three roles: gift steward, marketing enthusiast and technical expert.**

● **You must work with your board to establish gift stewardship and accountability guidelines for planned giving.** In chapter 6 I talked at length about the need to decide—in advance of starting your development program—what types of gifts you will accept, who will accept them, how you will valuate them, and how you will recognize them.

In addition, many potential planned-gift prospects and their financial advisors will want to know about your organization's fiduciary management policy and style. Does the staff make investment decisions, rely upon the guidance of a committee, or have an outside advisor? Is your investment philosophy conservative, middle-of-the-road, or visionary? What is your track record? Have you managed similar gifts?

● **You must acquire the specialized knowledge which assures prospects and their financial advisors that you can deal with the various planned-gift vehicles.** Whether you handle planned giving yourself or hire a staff person to specialize in it, a basic education in planned giving is necessary. There are several of excellent books—several of which are included in the resource bibliography at the end of this book—as well as newsletters and training programs on the subject. In addition, several states have professional associations which focus on planned giving and offer workshops and seminars regularly. Articles appear regularly in our professional magazines as well. Get yourself a good, basic education in the different kinds of vehicles—bequests, annuities and trusts, pooled income funds, using insurance, real estate, securities and other personal property—and acquire an understanding of the types of tax advantages they offer to your donors. With changing tax laws, even seasoned development officers need to review on a regular basis.

● **You must develop a full strategy that alerts prospects to your willingness to accept bequests and planned gifts.** Unfortunately, too many development directors simply concentrate on acquiring technical knowledge and rarely (or never) use it. The truth is that many of us feel uncomfortable talking to prospects about gift giving that involves confronting human mortality—we don't want to appear eager to benefit from our donor's death. We bury ourselves in technical minutiae and avoid talking to our prospects.

Because my own bias is a belief that the major role for the development officer is marketing bequest and planned gifts, the rest of this chapter is devoted to describing how to create a strategy that encourages potential donors to identify their interest.

A Commonsense Approach to Developing a Planned-Giving Marketing Scenario

■ **A fully developed bequest and planned-giving strategy will include the following components:**

> - **Communication pieces** that encourage people to "self-identify" their possible interest in making a bequest or planned gift.
>
> - **Seminars and workshops** that give more in-depth information. These should be done for both prospects and financial advisors.
>
> - **Appointments** with logical prospects to provide them with specific information on their particular situations.
>
> - **Expertise** either from a planned-giving advisory committee of experts—financial and legal—you can call upon for (free) advice and counsel or from a planned-giving consultant you can rely upon for (paid) advice and counsel.

■ **How aggressively you decide to market your program should depend on your analysis of the potential.** Because prospecting for bequest and planned gifts may have a delayed payoff to your organization you need to decide—before committing staff time, volunteer energies, and your limited budget—what the outcomes are likely to be.

While *all* not-for-profits should, at the least, alert their constituencies that bequests are always welcome, your organization might benefit from a more aggressive marketing program. Consider this if you meet any/all of the following criteria:

- Organizations with larger numbers of older donors have a better base of prospects than do those with mostly younger contributors

- Organizations which are perceived to have "made a difference" in prospect's lives are strongly positioned

- Organizations which have large numbers of steady, consistent annual donors have a good prospect base

- Organizations with a long-term, positive track record in the community and/or national recognition are more likely to be recommended by financial advisors

If you decide yours is an organization with minimal potential, you may want to only market passively, using communication vehicles that focus on bequests in the hope that your better prospects will self-identify. On the other hand, you might decide you have strong potential for planned gifts as well as bequest giving and want to strongly "nudge" your prospects with a more proactive marketing strategy.

■ **Your goal is to conduct your planned giving synergistically, using all available vehicles and moving from one step to another smoothly.** Here are the steps to consider, starting from least to most proactive:

● **Use all existing communication vehicles to heighten potential donor awareness.** *The simplest method of encouraging bequests and planned gifts involves placing "advertisements" in all existing organizational newsletters, annual reports, and* *performance/project programs as well as on the back side of all appeal reply vehicles.* Use your tracking system (chapter 8) to remind you of all the communications opportunities you have. Arrange to have copy placed in each and every one.

Create an advertisement you can use over and over again. Here is an example I especially like: Oregon Public Broadcasting targets its appeal to gratitude and moral obligation.

IF

... *Oregon Public Broadcasting has played an important role in making your life more enjoyable*

... *hardly a day goes by when you or a family member does not tune to Oregon Public Broadcasting*

... *you believe that OPB programming and other services should continue as strongly as possible*

OPB

THE GIFT

THAT KEEPS ON GIVING

Please consider including a bequest to the OPB Foundation in your will. Your gift will create a legacy of quality programming that enriches the lives of OPB audiences for generations to come. For more information, please complete the form below and return it to the OPB Foundation. Thank you.

Please send me more information about:

☐ Including a bequest for OPB in my will

☐ Making a gift of appreciated securities

☐ Making a gift through life insurance

☐ Generating income from my gift

• • • • • • • • • • •

☐ I have already included a bequest for OPB

☐ I plan to include a bequest for OPB in my will

CONFIDENTIAL REPLY

NAME

STREET

CITY

STATE   ZIP

PHONE

MAIL TO: Director of Planned Giving
OPB Foundation
PO Box 69485 - Portland, Oregon 97201
(503) 293-1935

Some organizations prefer to use a "question and answers" column dealing with financial planning or stories (thanking a donor, giving an example of goals met) on bequest

and planned giving in each vehicle. This has greater readability but requires more work on your part. Whichever format you
use—ongoing ads, financial columns, or stories—it must appear over and over again in your publications. It's been said it
takes five to seven times before a message is heard: aim for con-
sistency above art.

● **Identify your best prospects for bequests and planned gifts
and provide them with information on a regular schedule.** If
you want to move from the most passive form of marketing to a
more proactive stance, your next step is to divide out the
smaller group of prospects for bequests and planned gifts from
your larger prospect base. Typically, we use factors like age
(older), giving history (consistent), and closeness to organizations (volunteerism) to make some decisions. The beginning
section of this chapter may have given you additional ideas for
logical prospects within your organization's "family."

On a regular schedule—usually four times a year—send
these individuals a financial planning newsletter or brochure.
Focus on topics that address donors' goals, not the planned
giving methods. For example, end-of-calendar-year tax planning, retirement planning, saving for college, and estate planning are topics that interest larger numbers of individuals.
Some organizations try to prepare or purchase vehicles that address particular groups of prospects: the Stelter Company, a
planned-giving consulting firm from Des Moines, Iowa, offers
newsletters targeted to women and to older individuals.

You can buy vehicles from consultants or create your own.
For most organizations it makes sense to get these ready-made.
There are numerous vendors with vehicles ranging from four-
color, glossy newsletters to one-color, six-panel brochures. Request samples and compare for attractiveness, readability
(suggestion: look for larger type size!), and how relevant the
examples are to your organization and its prospects. If you do
decide to purchase newsletters or brochures be sure to find out
if any other not-for-profit in your area is using that series.

You may also want to have some follow-up brochures on
hand which explain various types of planned gifts in greater
detail. You can create your own brochures or buy them from
consultants. Don't get carried away and order large quantities.

If you get to the point with a prospect of discussing a specific method of planned giving, chances are you'll be doing this with the help of an advisor.

● **Offering workshops and financial planning seminars** is a logical next step for finding more active prospects for planned gifts. You can advertise such events to both your "family" audience and, using media announcements and advertisements, to the general public as well.

You need to have an articulate, knowledgeable presenter. One who knows both the field of financial planning and your organization. Some not-for-profits have this expertise among their board and volunteers; others must look for a consultant. In either case, the presenter must be someone who "bonds" with the audience. S/he must be able to make the audience relax, understand the material, and feel a sense of eagerness to make the world a better place through incorporating charitable giving into financial strategies. *If your presenter cannot do this, choose another.*

There are two additional key points to keep in mind:

Aim for quality, not for quantity. It really isn't important how many or how few individuals attend your workshop. What counts is the results: do you uncover bequests and/or help prospects to decide on a planned gift to your organization? In fact, large numbers can be a problem. I know a university planned-giving officer who drew more than one hundred and fifty attendees to a first financial-planning workshop. However, follow-up was non-existent and, as a result, the institution could not justify the costs for the event. A program with excellent potential was terminated.

A successful financial planning seminar solves needs of the attendees. There are two types of audiences which make sense: individuals and advisors. You need different types of workshops to attract each.

Very few individuals are interested in attending a workshop on "How to give your money away to a not-for-profit." The key financial concerns are: preparing for retirement, handling college expenses, and helping parents enjoy old age.

Other good topics include end-of-year planning for taxes and (general) estate planning. *Above all, while explaining options involving charitable giving will, of course, be a part of your presentation, it cannot be the entire focus.*

The Archdiocese of Seattle has been very successful in offering a series of financial planning seminars. But, even with a highly polished presentation and the close relationship between attendees and the church, bequests rose only from one to two percent.

The Office of Planned Giving determined that the problem was that many parishioners didn't have wills and were unwilling to go to an attorney to have wills prepared.

The Archdiocese changed its strategy. Instead, it offered complimentary will-writing sessions, using qualified volunteer attorneys, to a group of parishioners the Archdiocese felt would most benefit from this service.

Once an individual set an appointment, s/he received a reminder letter which also contained information about incorporating a bequest to the Church. Recorded expectancies rose by twenty-eight percent.

If your organization is ready and willing to accept more complex planned gifts, you'll want to work directly with financial advisors. They appreciate receiving information which will be of help to their clients. It's easy to get a list of advisors in your area: include C.P.A.s, bank trust officers, attorneys, insurance agents, financial planners, and tax advisors. There may be an organization of professionals concerned with estate planning in your area as well.

You need a real "pro" to attract these busy professionals. Be careful about using someone from the community: it may suggest favoritism. These events work best as quarterly breakfast meetings (easier to fit into busy schedules than luncheons) lasting exactly one and one-half hours. The format is 7:30–8:00 AM—networking and food; 8:00–8:45 AM—presentation; 8:45–9:00 AM information on your organization and its willingness to accept planned gifts. Consider topics such as "Retirement planning for the small business owner."

PORTLAND STATE
UNIVERSITY
FOUNDATION

January 7, 1988

Stephen S. McConnel
Moss, Adams
1001 S.W. Fifth #1400
Portland, OR 97204

Dear Mr. McConnel:

The enthusiastic response of Portland's financial advisors to our November workshop on tax planning has encouraged us to set a second workshop focusing on retirement planning.

The Tax Reform Act of 1986 has made it more difficult for business owners and others to save for retirement by limiting the deductibility of contributions to IRAs and other retirement plans. There are various ways to structure charitable trusts and annuity arrangements to help accumulate wealth and provide income for retirement.

On Wednesday, February 3, 1988 from 8:00 - 9:30 a.m., Portland State University will host a meeting of Portland-area financial advisors at the Portland Inn. You are invited to join your colleagues in discussing pertinent approaches to the changing tax climate.

Our presentor is J. Peter Wakeman, managing partner of the Westlake Village, California office of Helm & Purcell. Mr. Wakeman's practice is concentrated in the areas of charitable giving, taxation, estate planning and real estate. He is a member of the State Bars of California and Florida, the American Bar Association, the Los Angeles County Bar Association, and the Planned Giving Roundtable of Southern California. In addition, Mr. Wakeman has been appointed to a committee on charitable deductions sponsored by the American Bar Association.

We hope your schedule will permit you to attend. To help us with our planning, please RSVP by January 28, 1988 by calling Lois Wettstein at 464-4478.

Sincerely,

Harry L. Demorest
Managing Partner
Arthur Andersen & Co.

HLD:lw

- **Once an individual indicates s/he is interested in a possible bequest or planned gift, you need to follow up.** Call immediately. Try to set an appointment. The purpose of the appointment is to get to know your prospect better. What is s/he trying to accomplish? What are her/his needs? What is her/his financial lifestyle? It may take several meetings, involving experts and advisors, before the tentative outline of a planned gift evolves. Be patient! Experience has shown that those who make planned gifts also tend to increase their current giving to our organizations.

If you attempt to set a meeting and are told "no," send a follow-up letter and brochure reemphasizing how to make a bequest or planned gift to your organization and what it can accomplish. If you are planning any financial-planning seminars, let them know the date if it is set and follow up with an invitation. Often, it's the timing that's wrong. Don't hesitate to try to set another appointment after some weeks have passed.

If your prospect is the financial advisor, you will probably find yourself involved in exploratory meetings without knowing who the potential planned giver is. Respect the advisor's concern about staying in control.

- **Utilize expertise as needed.** The director of development need not be a technical expert but s/he should always know when to ask for advice. Because there are significant legal and tax implications involved in planned gifts never hesitate to call on either *qualified* volunteer or paid expertise to help you and your prospect. Few prospects expect you to be that knowledgeable about the specifics; rather they want you to be the "go-between."

My own preference is for paid expertise. First, the time involved with a planned-gift prospect can be extensive and, often, volunteers find it difficult to fit into busy schedules. Second, the focus must be on the benefit to the donor, not the organization. This is hard for volunteers to accept.

Increasingly, planned giving will be the path for securing major gift commitments. As individuals live longer (life expectancy for those born in the 1990s is 93 years of age!), their willingness to give up control of their assets when sixty, seventy, or eighty is likely to diminish. Bequests and planned giving will be increasingly accepted as the logical extension of current giving. Get prepared now.

PART V

ROUNDING OUT YOUR
FUND RAISING STRATEGY

While most of the potential for raising dollars is squarely with individuals, your organization will want to maximize its potential in *all* fund raising strategies.

In Chapter 17 we'll look at corporate giving patterns, corporate motivation, discuss finding corporate prospects, and using both the philanthropic and marketing approaches.

Chapter 18 looks at the trickle of gifts from the foundation sector and provides guidance in deciding how much effort to put into this area of funding, as well as some help in choosing foundation prospects, and a look at the art of grantsmanship.

We'll end in chapter 19 with a discussion of special-event fund raising, placed—rightfully—as the last development strategy of choice.

CHAPTER SEVENTEEN

The Challenge of Corporate Giving

*E*IGHTY-FOUR PERCENT of chief executive officers from the top 1,000 companies agree that enlightened self-interest must guide corporate giving. They're backing it up with their giving strategies: more tied to marketing, more focused, and more reflective of employee concerns.

Gene Wilson, President of the ARCO Foundation, states bluntly that "Corporate giving is strategic giving." Lee Katz, Executive Vice-President of the American Associates of Ben Gurion University, concurs. She notes that corporations are required to function as bottom-line organizations. They must, in effect, achieve a *bang for the buck*. Therefore, "mutual benefit must be the essential ingredient in any successful proposal to a corporation."

Writing in the June 1990 issue of *Fund Raising Management* magazine, Ms. Katz suggests that corporate logically goes to communities in those geographic locations having a concentration of corporate employees and business affiliations. Additionally, your organization needs to demonstrate itself as being capable of:

- Enriching or enhancing the quality of life for employees

- Addressing priority concerns the corporation

has defined for itself, often related to its product line, e.g., health, agriculture, medicine

- Being represented by individuals or groups who enjoy special relationships with the corporation's leadership, i.e., members of the board, major stockholders, high-level officers

- Achieving positive public relations visibility

- Providing large numbers of employees for the corporation's workforce pool

- Training or retraining employees for the corporation's specific manpower needs

THE SHRINKING CORPORATE CONTRIBUTIONS PIE

Although America's business leaders say they remain committed to the concept of corporate philanthropy, most admit they are not optimistic about increased giving in the 1990s. An anticipated harsher business climate—including bottom-line pressures, changes in ownership and mergers, and a "lean and mean" approach to management—suggests that the days of major gains are over.

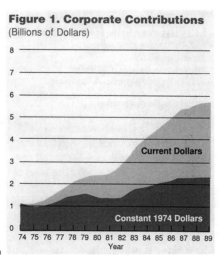

Figure 1. Corporate Contributions
(Billions of Dollars)

Source: CFAE, 1990

Until 1986, charitable giving by U.S. corporations increased by an average of about 10 percent a year for nearly fifty
years. Since then, contributions have leveled off: corporate
charitable contributions in the United States rose to $5.9 bil-
lion in 1990, a relatively modest increase from the $5.6 billion
of 1989 and a continuation of the slowdown that began in 1988,
when giving rose 2 percent to $5.4 billion.

Is Your Organization a Corporate Priority?

■ **Corporate giving trends have remained fairly constant.** In
1974, 37 percent of corporate contributions were given to educational institutions; in 1989, the percentage had increased to
38.8 percent.
  In descending order, corporate support went as follows:

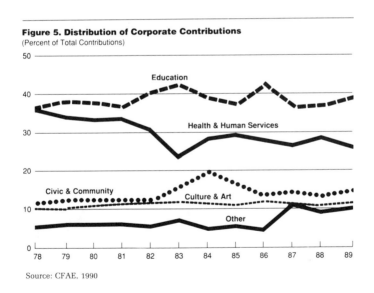

Figure 5. Distribution of Corporate Contributions
(Percent of Total Contributions)

Source: CFAE, 1990

■ **How likely is *your* not-for-profit to receive a corporate gift?** In
a comprehensive survey of 1,600 companies, the descending
order of popularity for support was as follows:

Category	Percent
Private Colleges	94.8%
General Education	93.2%
United Way	63.7%
Fine Arts Institutes	52.3%
Cultural Institutes	50.2%
Civic Programs	49.3%
Minority Programs	48.8%
National Organizations	43.0%
Youth Service	42.3%
Federated Campaigns	33.3%
General Arts	33.1%
International	32.4%
Public Colleges	31.6%
Scholarships	31.3%
Music	29.9%
Urban Problems	29.7%
Theatre	29.4%
General Health Care	28.5%
Economic Education	28.4%
Economic Development	27.7%
Welfare Programs	26.6%
Environmental	22.8%
Dance	22.4%
Hospitals	22.3%
Community Arts	21.8%
Rural Issues	21.7%
Medical Research	21.1%
Elem./Secondary Ed.	20.0%
Job Development	19.8%
Public Broadcasting	19.2%

General Charitable	19.1%
Children's Programs	17.5%
Women's Programs	16.8%
Vocational Ed.	15.7%
Legal Services	13.1%
Justice/Ex-offenders	10.8%
Film	9.5%
Science	8.8%
Handicapped/Disabled	7.6%
Political	7.6%
United Way Agencies	7.4%
Legal Advocacy	7.3%
Community Organizing	7.1%
Equal Rights	6.8%
Scientific Research	4.6%
Continuing Education	3.9%
Science Education	3.9%
Neighborhood Based	3.6%
Senior Citizens	3.1%
Religious/Non-sect.	2.9%
Religious/Sectarian	2.9%
Writing and Poetry	2.1%
Family Life	2.0%
Humanities	1.9%
Redevelopment	1.6%
Alcohol/Drug Treatment	1.4%
Occupational Health	.9%
Sports	.4%
Non Tax-Exempt	.2%
Gay/Lesbian Programs	.1%

Source: Sam Sternberg, National Directory of Corporate Charity (San Francisco: Regional Young Adult Project, 1984)

While it is probable that some areas at the bottom half of the corporate charity list will gain support in the 1990s (elementary/secondary education, job development, handicapped/disabled, continuing education, and senior citizens appear most likely as per the reasons given in chapter 2), the overall priorities are not likely to change.

Unless your not-for-profit falls in the top percentile grouping, corporate funding is a long shot at best.

■ **With less than 5 percent of gifts available from the corporate giving pocket, you need to identify your targets carefully.** Some industries are more charitably inclined than others; some target giving to specific types of not-for-profits. *Target your research to those corporations who are most likely to give to your type of not-for-profit.*

● **Begin your research with your own local corporations.** Most communities have a number of local business publications and networking meetings. Subscribe to the weekly newspaper, order the monthly magazine, attend the chamber of commerce and city club meetings regularly. Develop a file on each corporation: request the annual reports, copies of internal newsletters, clip articles of relevance. Identify a top-level contact person at those corporations you want to approach and work to cultivate that person—both for personal giving and for endorsement of your cause to the company.

● **Don't forget smaller businesses.** Many not-for-profits ignore the professional services businesses and entrepreneurial businesses. This is a serious mistake. Given the actual dollars you will probably get from your major corporate prospect, the smaller business may be a better choice for cultivation! You'll be able to deal immediately with the top decision-maker and s/he is often overlooked by other non-profits as both a volunteer and a contributor.

● **Concentrate your national efforts on your best prospects.** Your organization may not, in fact, have any logical prospects away from its own back yard. Success requires:

having access (through a board member or other "door opener") to the appropriate company representative

and

having a similar profile (as demonstrated in the charts in this chapter) to other funded not-for-profits

● **Learn the type of funding that corporations are likely to do within each area of support:**

Corporate Giving, 1988

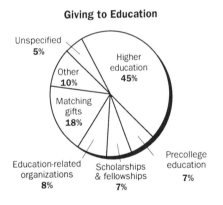

Giving to Education

Unspecified 5%
Other 10%
Higher education 45%
Matching gifts 18%
Education-related organizations 8%
Scholarships & fellowships 7%
Precollege education 7%

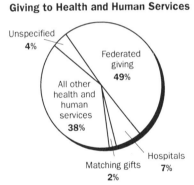

Giving to Health and Human Services

Unspecified 4%
Federated giving 49%
All other health and human services 38%
Matching gifts 2%
Hospitals 7%

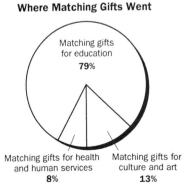

Where Matching Gifts Went

Matching gifts for education 79%
Matching gifts for health and human services 8%
Matching gifts for culture and art 13%

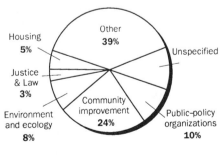

Giving to Civic and Community Activities

Housing 5%
Other 39%
Unspecified
Justice & Law 3%
Community improvement 24%
Environment and ecology 8%
Public-policy organizations 10%

REQUESTING THE CORPORATE GIFT

■ **Your formal proposal should be the last step in the cultivation and solicitation cycle of a corporate prospect.** Burnell R. Roberts, chairman and CEO of Mead Corporation recommends not-for-profits "educate your (corporate) donors about your organization and how you are working to meet community needs. To be blunt about it, don't knock on the door only when you need a donation."

In chapter 3 we talked about maintaining the balance between what your donors expect from you and what you want from them. Your corporate donors are not faceless entities: the individuals who represent these organizations want you to communicate consistently with them and to build a relationship of mutual respect and trust.

Says Roberts: "That means you'll have to do a better job of *listening* to donors; you'll have to expect to answer *tough* questions; you'll have to *understand* who I am and what my interests are; and you'll have to do a better job of *offering solutions* that I can support to meet community needs."

■ **Before you formally ask for corporate support**

- Make certain the cause or program you're asking the corporation to support is worthy by community standards, not simply a "pet project" of a small group or an individual.

- Tell the corporation what funding alternatives you've considered and what types of support you need including volunteers, publicity, matching dollars.

- Provide ideas for maximizing the corporation's contribution and/or employee involvement. Think about using challenge grants, for example.

- Make sure the operating costs of your organization are in line. Most corporations are more interested in providing the initial funding for start-up projects or seed money for new ideas.

- Know what the corporation is supporting already and where your proposal fits in.

- Make certain you identify a strong common interest between your organization's request and the company.

- Be prepared to show strong involvement by members of your board and, if possible, by company employees.

- Make sure your proposal is well thought-out and professionally presented.

MARKETING OR PHILANTHROPY?

■ **Often, the marketing arm of the company—through sponsorships and underwriting—is a stronger approach than the philanthropic arm.** Profit-motivated giving (more frequently called cause-related marketing, a term copyrighted by the Travel-Related Services unit of the American Express Company) is the area of growth for many corporations and, increasingly, for smaller businesses as well. Just as with the philanthropic arm, you need to research whether your organization is likely to receive funding and limit your proposals to the most likely corporate candidates.

■ **A key to using cause-related marketing properly is to "know your partners' needs."** Warner Canto, vice president, special projects for American Express, rightfully decries the many cause-related marketing programs that have been "poorly conceived," featuring "inappropriate causes" and "ill-defined objectives." He urges businesses to apply the same marketing disciplines to cause-related marketing programs as they do to other marketing efforts and called for not-for-profits to become better marketers.

■ **Guidelines for cause-related marketing** have been developed by the Council of Better Business Bureaus' Philanthropic Advisory Service. Here are nine suggestions for businesses and charities considering participation in joint-venture marketing:

1. Is the charity familiar with the participating corporation's subsidiaries, products and/or services?

2. Is the corporation informed about the participating charity's programs, finances, and other fund raising efforts?

3. Is there a written agreement that gives formal permission for the corporation to use the charity's name and logo?

4. Does the written agreement: (a) give the charity prior review and approval of ad materials that use its name, (b) indicate how long the campaign will last, (c) specify how and when charitable funds will be distributed, (d) explain any steps that will be taken in case of a disagreement or unforeseen result with the promotion?

5. Do the joint-venture advertisements: (a) specify the actual or anticipated portion of the sales or service price to benefit the charity, (b) indicate the full name of the charity, (c) include an address or phone number to contact for additional information about the charity or the campaign, (d) indicate when the campaign will end

and, if applicable, the maximum amount the charity will receive?

6. Does the promotion follow all applicable state regulations in the areas the marketing will take place? Some states now have specific guidelines for sales made in conjunction with charities.

7. Does the corporation have fiscal controls in place to process and record the monies received to benefit the charity?

8. Will more than one charity be involved in the promotion? If so, how will funds be distributed?

9. Will the corporation complete a financial report at the end of the campaign (or annually, if the campaign lasts more than a year), which identifies (a) the total amount collected for the charity, (b) any campaign expenses, and (c) how much the charity received?

Whether you're aiming for the company contributions committee or the company's marketing director, corporate contributions requires an aggressive strategy. You must be fully knowledgeable about what your future partner needs and wants. Only then are you likely to succeed.

CHAPTER EIGHTEEN

The Fountain of Foundation Funding: Can You Get More than a Trickle?

DOING YOUR *"HOMEWORK"* is the key to foundation grants. You must know what types of organizations the foundation supports, whether it will make operating, program-specific, capital or endowment grants, if the foundation provides one-time or multi-year commitments, makes restricted or unrestricted gifts, puts geographical limitations on its gifts, and the range of gifts it will make.

Foundation support accounts for less than 6 percent of the philanthropic dollar, amounting to just a little over $7.08 billion of a total $122.57 billion in 1990.

WHO'S GIVING WHAT?

■ **Foundation giving is heavily weighted towards educational institutions and other groups involved in education.** In 1989, for example, they received 39.6 percent of foundation dollars. Colleges, universities, and graduate schools received over $1 billion, or 31.8 percent of the total.

■ **More and more foundation grants are going to provide specific program support, rather than for general operating support,** according to a report by the Foundation Center. Program support reached a five-year high, accounting for nearly 43 percent of the grants and 46 percent of grant dollars while general support dipped to a five-year low, at 11.3 percent of grant dol-

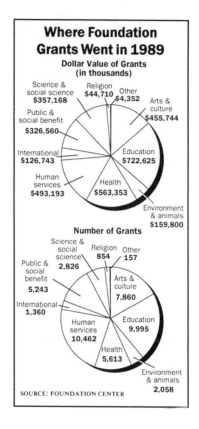

Where Foundation Grants Went in 1989

Dollar Value of Grants (in thousands)

- Science & social science $357,168
- Religion $44,710
- Other $4,352
- Arts & culture $455,744
- Public & social benefit $326,560
- International $126,743
- Education $722,625
- Human services $493,193
- Health $563,353
- Environment & animals $159,800

Number of Grants

- Science & social science 2,826
- Religion 854
- Other 157
- Public & social benefit 5,243
- Arts & culture 7,860
- International 1,360
- Education 9,995
- Human services 10,462
- Health 5,613
- Environment & animals 2,058

SOURCE: FOUNDATION CENTER

lars and 16.2 percent of grants, according to the 1990-91 edition of the *Foundation Grants Index*, which covers grants made in 1989. Most of the remainder went for capital projects, research, and student aid.

■ **The leadership at foundations is changing and patterns of support are changing with it.** Since 1988, a large number of the major private and community foundations have appointed new CEOs. The *Chronicle of Philanthropy* notes that ''of the 100 wealthiest foundations alone, one quarter have new leadership, including seven of the top ten. And many smaller funds have new people in charge of their day-to-day operations.'' Most of the new leadership are younger—many are *baby boomers*, born between 1946 and 1964. They come into their present posts from outside the foundation world. Most significantly, they hold the values of the 1960s: optimism tempered by distrust of large established institutions, a belief in consensus building and grassroots participation, and a strong desire to make a difference. Three concerns predominate: the environmental crisis, the growing gap between the rich and the poor, and the deterioration of the public schools.

■ **The pattern of past foundation giving suggests the following continuing trends:**

- More large grants to fewer organizations

- More giving to education, especially for elementary schools and secondary schools, with grants to higher education remaining constant

- More grants for the environment and protection of animals

- More grants for projects for women and girls

- More grants for mental health and the prevention and treatment of specific diseases including AIDS

- More emphasis on community issues and social services

- More grants to arts and cultural organizations but with increased competition among such organizations

- Fewer grants in the sciences

GETTING YOUR SHARE OF FOUNDATION FUNDING

According to foundation officials, giving away money is hard work. They complain that their organizations are overwhelmed with poorly prepared requests, flooded with computer-generated proposals and accused of biases by disappointed grantseekers.

Today foundations say they are looking for:

- Closer working relationships between grantmakers and grant recipients

and

- Increased emphasis on holding recipients accountable for proper management and use of funds and on foundation review of the long-term benefits of programs

■ **Begin your research with local foundations.** There is a definite geographical clustering of grantmakers and grantees. The greatest numbers of grants and grant dollars are given by foundations to not-for-profits in their own communities: New York and California (with 102 and 52 foundations respectively) far outpace other areas in both giving and getting.

Your local United Way or a similar organization probably produces a guide to area foundations. It's important to have a current guide: new foundations are being started all the time; trustees change; emphases shift.

■ **Ask for appropriate grant amounts.** The typical foundation has $600,000 in assets—a far cry from the giants like Ford, Rockefeller, and Carnegie. Review previous grants in their annual reports and tax forms (available through the Foundation Center—see the Resource Bibliography). Look for patterns of support dollars.

■ **Limit your national efforts to realistic prospects.** The computer has been a boon to grantseekers and a torment to grantmakers. It is so tempting to just change the name of the foundation and send out one more proposal. Foundation officers complain they are drowning in inappropriate proposal paper. Save a tree—don't add to the clutter.

REQUESTING THE FOUNDATION GIFT

■ **Do you only communicate with foundation prospects when you want money?** That's the pattern at too many not-for-profits. Make sure you add appropriate foundations to your mailing list to receive newsletters and/or magazines, annual reports, press releases, copies of your brochures and appeals. Keep in touch through phone calls; invite representatives to your events.

Rather than develop a huge list of foundation prospects you don't cultivate, hone your pool to the best ten to twenty and continuously involve them with your organization.

The steps we mentioned under corporate giving (chapter 17) are mostly valid for foundations as well. With modest changes:

- Make certain the cause or program you're asking the foundation to support is worthy by community standards, not simply a "pet project" of a small group or an individual.

- Tell the foundation what funding alternatives you've considered and what types of support you need.

- Provide ideas for maximizing the foundation's contribution. Think about asking for a challenge grant or "seed" money for hiring a development consultant to give your program a jump-start.

- Make sure the operating costs of your organization are covered. Most foundations are more interested in providing specific program support than general funding.

- Know what the foundation is supporting already and where your proposal fits in.

- Make certain you identify a strong common interest between your organization's request and the foundation.

- Be prepared to show strong support by your "family" before going to a foundation.

- Make sure your proposal follows the guidelines for timing and content. Don't send a book if a letter will do.

Unlike their counterparts in the corporation, whose giving is heavily linked to a quantifiable marketing strategy, foundation officers' goals are often broader in scope. Presented properly, a proposal that promises dramatic results can receive a warm reception. Follow the steps recommended in this chapter to set the stage for that welcome.

CHAPTER NINETEEN

The Do's and Don'ts of Special Events

SPECIAL EVENTS CAN BE either
for friend raising, where the goal is to involve large numbers of
volunteers and participants for image-building reasons, or for
fund raising, where the goal is to raise large dollars as efficiently as possible. While a very few events combine elements
of both successfully, most organizations think they are doing
fund raising when they are actually involved in friend raising.

Special events belong last on any fund raiser's list. They di-
vert energies from more productive fund raising and, typically,
don't raise significant money. In addition, they may confuse or
even anger donors who treat their ticket costs as contributions.
Yet often, when fund raising is necessary, we decide to hold a
special event. Why? Perhaps because it appears to be a less
threatening form of raising money than a direct ask.

The bottom line on special events is often overlooked. The
"profit" should be calculated as the income remaining after
you subtract both the cost of staff and volunteer time and of the
event itself. Once you have the expense and income figures,
check the rate-of-return ratio. *Special events are the most
costly of fund raising vehicles!* Typically, charities spend 30 to
60 percent of receipts on the cost of the event.

**Does this mean you shouldn't include special events in your
development plan?** That depends: if your organization already
has an event with which it is identified look at the potential for
maximizing the dollars raised. Or, a unique opportunity may
present itself which makes perfect (dollars and) sense!

■ **Successful special events fund raising requires three specifics:** a constituency of high potential, a strong chair and committee, and a gap in the community calendar of events. Marie-Jo Dulade-Coclet, a fund development consultant for Girl Scouts of the USA, emphasizes that key to the success of your special event is finding "the party animal or animals" in the community. If they aren't enthusiastic and supportive, your event won't go.

And, special events seem to attract a wide range of pitfalls and problems. Personally, I've dealt with the wrath of nature (an event in conflict with the Blizzard of 1976), guests of honor who either "forget" the date or show up late, food problems ranging from too little to too bad, and so forth.

Regardless of cause, the results reflect on your organization. Charles P. Anderson, Director of Development at Hospice Care of Rhode Island, and Anne Garnett, Director of Development at Save The Bay, caution that "improper planning, lack of contingency plans, and even acts of God can cause a laudable effort to backfire with terrible results."

■ **There are all kinds of special events.** Here is an excellent guide to factors to consider which was developed by Charles Anderson and Anne Garnett.

SPECIAL EVENT CHECK LIST

Event	Volunteer Intensive Y or N	Expenses L-Large M-Moderate S-Small	Professional Help Needed Y or N	Audience General/ Targeted	Benefits	Potential Problems
WALK-A-THON TYPE	Y	S	N	General	1. Vol. Involvement 2. Public Relations 3. $$	1. Weather 2. Lack of Participation 3. Undesirable Route
RAFFLES (Small, Donated Prizes)	Y	S	N	General	1. Vol. Involvement 2. Low (No) Risk 3. Limited $$	1. Undesirable Prize(s) 2. Low Participation
RAFFLES (Limited Entry)	N	L	N	Targeted	1. Large $$ 2. Public Relations	1. Front Loaded 2. Must Cover Expenses 3. Over-Priced Tickets 4. Lack of Participation
GOLF TOURNEYS	Y	L	Y	Targeted	1. Vol. Involvement 2. $$	1. Weather 2. Limited Participation 3. Liquor Liability
AUCTIONS	Y	M+	Y	General	1. Vol. Involvement 2. $$	1. Auctioneer 2. Items for Sale 3. Liquor Liability
CONCERTS	Y	L	Y	General/ Targeted	1. Vol. Involvement 2. $$ 3. Public Relations	1. No-Shows 2. Acoustics 3. Front Loaded
COCKTAIL PARTIES	N	M	N	Targeted	1. $$ 2. Donor Cultivation	1. Bad Timing 2. Low Attendance 3. Liquor Liability
ROASTS, TRIBUTE DINNERS	Y	L	Y	Targeted	1. $$ 2. Vol. Involvement 3. Public Relations 4. Donor Cultivation	1. Prestige of Guest 2. Timing 3. No-Shows 4. Liquor Liability
DINNER DANCES	Y	L	Y	Targeted	1. $$ 2. Public Relations 3. Donor Cultivation	1. Timing 2. Poor Attendance 3. Liquor Liability 4. Poor Food (Band)

"UMBRELLA" FUND RAISING FOR SPECIAL EVENTS

If, after evaluating the concerns about special events fund raising I have advanced, you decide to go ahead with an event, *make a vow to bring many different possibilities for fund raising under its "umbrella."* By doing this, you will maximize the dollars you can raise even if your event is not a high-profile one. Once again, we are utilizing the concept of synergy.

Special events income comes from three main sources.

- Ticket Sales

- Advertising and Underwriting

- Auxiliary Events

■ **Ticket sales** should cover basic expenses for your event. This means you need to be realistic as to pricing. Don't fall into the trap of pricing your tickets low in the hopes of attracting a larger audience and expecting other areas of revenue to make up the shortfall. Be sure you have thought out your expense budget fully before recommending ticket pricing. I like to use a "worse case," conservative, and optimistic income projection as part of my planning process.

There are a number of things you can do to increase revenues from ticket sales. They include:

● *Offer an early bird discount for advance reservations.* This works especially well when your event has a high cost attached to it. An incentive can give your organization some early cash flow to cover expenses.

● *Invite your better prospects to become Benefactors and Patrons of the event.* This is similar to the Donor Recognition concept in that the emphasis is put on leadership as opposed to getting more back from your contribution. Benefactors and

Patrons can be listed in your event's program as a nice touch of appreciation.

● *Get the publicity out as early and as widely as possible.* Use "save the date" and teaser copy in your organization's own communication vehicles. As soon as you know your event will be in the spring (even if the exact date isn't firmed up), begin your announcements. Build the excitement by releasing a series of more complex announcements prior to the actual invitation.

● *Create a large committee and urge everyone to come as a paying guest.* Make it a ground rule, brought up formally at your first or second planning meeting, that freebies will be strictly limited. Put this in your minutes. Then, extend the early bird's lower price to all staff and volunteers as a courtesy.

● *Sell blocks of tickets to corporations, organizations, even your committee members at the early bird price.* It becomes their responsibility to resell the tickets. Doing this gives you guaranteed income but may result in many no-shows. Weigh the advantages and disadvantages carefully.

You can also consider inviting another not-for-profit to share in the benefits of your event by promoting tickets on your behalf.

There are logical reasons for a youth organization, for example, to encourage participation in events that strengthen the programs of substance abuse, self-esteem, health, and environmental organizations. Depending on what risks they also share, your partner organization can receive a percentage of the gate.

● *Don't forget your honorees.* They have family, friends, and business acquaintances who should receive an early announcement of your event. Don't forget that the members of your committee and board are also being honored for their work in making your event and your organization a success. Ask for their lists as well. This works especially well if board and committee names are listed on the invitation.

■ **Advertising and underwriting** can bring in more dollars than the event itself. But, both need to be carefully planned out and initiated *a year in advance* of the event to allow time for your prospects to consider and accept.

Neither advertising nor underwriting should be viewed as philanthropy. In many cases the decision to do or not will be linked to marketing objectives and will come out of your advertiser or underwriter's advertising/marketing budget. (A full discussion of cause-related marketing can be found in chapter 15). You need to sell participation as a logical way to access new audiences and/or reaffirm linkage to current audiences.

● *Articulate what you are offering clearly, in marketing terms.* What are the demographics (size, age, sex, income, household make-up, education, religious/ethnic background, geographical distribution, etc.) of the potential audience? Any possible "pass-along" readership or participation? Your initial letter of inquiry should clearly indicate the advantages to placing an ad or being associated as an underwriter of the event.

● *Don't give away the shop!* Set your fees at a level that reflects the uniqueness and quality of the audience you can provide. Check to see what other organizations and for-profit vehicles are charging for similar opportunities.

● *Develop a handout sheet* that can be inserted with your letter of inquiry or used alone, if necessary, listing all options with stipulations for payment in advance. Define what an advertiser and underwriter gets: must ads, for example, be camera ready or will you do any typesetting other than name and address? Are underwriters given free tickets (how many) or other special treatment?

● *Offer different levels of advertising and underwriting.* A program journal lends itself to advertising, large and small. Offer your supporters their choice of full-page, half-page, quarter-page, business-card sized, and "booster" (one-line listing) advertisements. You can charge premiums for covers and the two-page centerspread. I've added in gold and silver pages for anniversary dinner dances. Especially lucrative are the "booster" pages which can contain, under a common heading of Best Wishes, hundreds of names. Consider adding a line onto your invitation response vehicle to encourage listings.

Similarly, with underwriting, define levels such as full sponsor, co-sponsor, supporting sponsors, etc. Be ready to provide potential sponsors with specifics of how one level differs from the other. Start with your best prospect and try to get a commitment for full sponsorship. If that's not possible, work down the levels.

● *It's important that you use appropriate lists.* You'll want to let all the members of your "family" know about these additional opportunities to demonstrate their support. But, don't stop there! Every organization has access to additional, logical advertisers and underwriters including:

Lists provided by honorees including both personal and business acquaintances. As with ticket sales, use lists from board and committee members as well.

Vendors and suppliers to your organization and to organizations affiliated with your "family" members. It's especially useful if you can indicate in your contact letter or call that this is not only an opportunity to support an organization your vendor has benefited from but to also increase awareness of their products and services.

Major corporations are your best source of major underwriting. A full list of local businesses is usually available from the business newspaper. Recognize that major corporations commit the dollars from the marketing budget based on goals, not sentiment. Be prepared to state your case in their terms.

Professionals—doctors, dentists, accountants, attorneys— are all listed in the Yellow Pages or can be found through their professional societies. They are outstanding prospects for business-card ads in your journal.

Small businesses can be found through your Small Business Development Center and women and minority networking organizations. They, too, are good prospects for business-card ads.

■ **Auxiliary events** are often overlooked by organizations as they plan special events. Simply put, this refers to trying to include under your special event's "umbrella" any additional sources of revenue that make sense. Often these are "day of event" activities which are modestly priced. They might include:

- raffles and door-prize drawings

- silent or oral auction of one or two special prizes

- a store at the event selling memorabilia or organizational merchandise

- an information booth that has donor recognition and membership forms available

- photographs sold to commemorate the event

- "pre" and "after" event add-ons such as a champagne reception or a lavish coffee and dessert finale

- food booths for non-food events

- tapes of the event's entertainment or speeches (usually sent afterwards but signed up for at event)

While I maintain that for most not-for-profits the time and energy spent on special events is better put into the cultivation and solicitation of a targeted prospect group, following the suggestions of this chapter can maximize the dollars you will raise.

PART VI
EVALUATING YOUR DEVELOPMENT PLAN

Too often, development officers get so caught up in the day-to-day business of raising money that they lose sight of the larger picture. Every so often, it's important to make the time to check how you're doing.

Chapter 20 explains the concept of environmental scanning, introducing the *development audit*. Auditing can help your organization:

> —capitalize on early opportunities rather than lose these to competitors
> —receive an early signal of impending problems which can be defused if recognized well in advance
> —sensitize volunteers and staff to the changing needs of the organization's constituencies
> —access a base of objective qualitative information about the environment you can use in your planning and which will stimulate your thinking
> —evaluate the need to improve the image of the organization with its public by analyzing how sensitive and responsive it is to its environment
> —provide a means of continuing, broad-based education for the management team

Chapter 21 is a generic version of a survey I developed for my own consulting. You are welcome to use this as a starting point for your own evaluation efforts.

CHAPTER TWENTY

The Audit: An Evaluation Tool

CONGRATULATIONS! YOU'VE DE-
FINED your development strategy, developed your fund raising
methodologies, are working the synergies and tracking the
results. Now, you need to evaluate your results.

■ **The development audit is a specialized form of "environmental scanning" that enables not-for-profits to approach fund
raising both effectively and efficiently.** The purpose of the development audit is to help you choose where you will concentrate your efforts so you can maximize your fund development
program, given realistic staffing and budget constraints.

The development audit assumes that you need to pause to
look objectively at what is currently happening (and not happening). Your organization may be confused about what its development plan should and could be. The development audit
helps achieve consensus among board members, administrative and development staff.

Robert J. Berendt and J. Richard Taft in their book, *How to
Rate Your Development Office,* suggest a number of questions
you must be able to answer if you want to have a strong development program:

- Where are we today and what are we selling to the public, to our members and donors?

- Is what we are today what we want to be tomorrow?

- Do our potential publics perceive us in the same manner we perceive ourselves?

- Do they, by and large, approve of our work and endorse our objectives for tomorrow?

- What kinds of financial resources will we need to finance the objectives we have in mind for tomorrow?

- What are our financial priorities in everything from construction to program funds?

- Are the people in our institution behind our vision and do they understand the goals ahead?

- With whom are we competing, and is there anything particularly unique or distinctive about our approach to the field?

- How do we best communicate our distinctions, goals, and objectives to our publics?

- Where do our trustees and volunteers fit in?

- How do roles of management, trustees, and staff complement each other in the marketing, membership and development processes?

Answering these questions is the heart of the audit. In doing so, the development audit focuses on:

> —evaluating what is currently being done both by your organization and any competition
> —realistically assessing what is the potential for raising monies from different audiences
> —outlining strategy steps and tools to get from one to the other as quickly and cost effectively as possible

The audit's findings and recommendations are based on a review of internal materials and relevant external materials, as well as meetings held with members of the board, key volunteers, community leaders, program participants, and staff.

The end result is a written report (see box) with three main parts:

● **The Executive Summary** gives the key findings of the audit in summary form. It identifies the three to four areas of concern, generally and specifically to fund raising, that need to be addressed.

● **The Overview** explains the "climate." It sets forth what is happening nationally and locally, how the organization is perceived by current and potential funding constituencies, and summarizes what are the strengths and areas of concern that impact on raising money successfully. It will help with realistic goal setting and enable the council to continuously evaluate how well the program is proceeding.

● **The Strategic Recommendations Section** outlines the current development and related efforts and indicates what necessary components are missing. It provides clear, realistic recommendations for moving the development program along.

An audit evaluates the historical. This allows you to be honest about your past fund raising. You must look at all facets of your development strategy (annual giving, major and planned giving, special events as well as corporate and foundation relations) and recommends steps under image building, board development, public relations, donor acknowledgement and recognition, community outreach, and sponsorship and promotional scenarios. If your organization raises funds through membership, ticket, program or product sales you need to look at these areas as well.

**A COMPREHENSIVE ASSESSMENT
OF THE FUND RAISING POTENTIAL
OF "ABC" ORGANIZATION**
prepared by Judith E. Nichols, CFRE

PURPOSE OF THE DEVELOPMENT AUDIT

EXECUTIVE SUMMARY

DETAILED OVERVIEW: The Climate for Fund Raising
- What's happening
  - nationally
  - locally
- How is "ABC" Organization perceived?
- A Summary of the Strengths and Areas of Concern Impacting on Fund Raising

STRATEGIC RECOMMENDATIONS
- Setting Fund Raising Goals
- Specific Recommendations for Related Areas
  - Goal Setting
  - Board Development
  - Imaging
  - Membership/Program
- Specific Recommendations for Fund Raising
  - Gift Recognition/Acknowledgement
  - Annual Fund
  - Major Gifts
  - Planned Giving

•Special Events
•Corporate and Foundation Relations
APPENDICES
   – Audit Survey
   – Community Resources from United Way
   – Demographic Material

■ **Should you do your own audit?** You can. While many organizations bring in consultants to conduct development audits, a seasoned development officer can handle the audit her/himself. Let's look at the pros and cons:

PRO

- You know the organization's history.

- You understand the strengths and weaknesses of various staff members, board members, etc.

- You know the "climate": is the organization likely to move quickly, slowly?

- You'll save the costs of hiring a consultant.

CON

- You may be "learning on the job," too junior to feel confident in suggesting bold changes of direction.

- You are too busy dealing with hands-on fund raising responsibility to make the time.

- You're uncomfortable saying the things that need to be said.

- You may be part of the problem.

■ **Doing an audit requires a commitment of time and effort.** Regardless of whether you decide to do your audit yourself or use a consultant, gathering the necessary information will take a considerable amount of input from the staff and the board.

If you decide to use a consultant, s/he should have an audit survey form personalized for your organization. When you interview consultants, look for those who have conducted audits previously on organizations similar in size and scope to yours. Find out what will be included and how long the process will take.

■ **The Nichols' Audit.** For your use either in evaluating proposals from consultants or in doing your own audit, you can review a generic form of the development audit I provide for my clients in the next chapter.

Don't be overwhelmed by the quantity of information requested. And, don't be concerned if your response is ''none'' or ''not available'' to any questions; that's part of the audit process.

Once you've decided on the audit format you want to use, you'll need to set appointments with members of the staff and key volunteers: you might include your executive director, other fund raising staff, as well as your membership coordinator, product sales coordinator, and program directors if appropriate. I also recommend meeting with local civic and community leaders who are **not** currently involved with your organization as well as some who are.

Organize the information you gather along the lines I've suggested (Executive Summary, Detailed Overview, and Strategic Recommendations) or whatever makes most sense for you.

Focus on substance, not style. The audit need not be a deathless work of prose. You can choose to make your points in outline style rather than narrative.

Finally, recognize that the results should be a collaborative effort. ''Ownership'' should be given to everyone who has had input. I conduct as broad a debriefing as an organization can handle. Both staff and board members need to be involved.

Good luck!

CHAPTER TWENTY-ONE

Nichols' Generic Fund Raising Audit

THE SURVEY ON THIS and the following pages is a general version of the questionnaire I use in conjunction with my auditing. Each organization must personalize the audit according to its specific concerns and needs but my version is a good starting point.

I. MISSION, LEADERSHIP, AND IMAGE

A. DEMOGRAPHIC BACKGROUND
   (RESOURCES: Census Bureau, chamber of commerce, United Way)
   a. Define area demographics:
      • What is expected population growth through 2000?
         – Is make-up (by sex, racial/ethnic background, age, education, etc.) changing?
         – Is youth increasing, decreasing, stable?
      • How is population doing economically?
         – Are there pockets of affluence?
         – Is the region prospering, depressed?
   b. Define organizational demographics and other characteristics:
      • Number of members/clients served
         – growth rate? retention rate?
      • Number of sites?

B. CLIMATE FOR FUND RAISING
   a. How many not-for-profits are in area?
      • any direct competition to organization?
      • any major fund raising campaigns?
      • how sophisticated is the fund raising?
   b. How does United Way see the funding trends?
      • projected allocations over three years?
      • projected areas of interest?
      • what are the regulations? any changes coming?
   c. Where can potential dollars come from? In what formats?
      (cash, volunteer help, gifts-in-kind)
      • Community Foundations?
      • Area Foundations?
      • Local Businesses?
      • National Foundations/Corporations?
      • Individuals?
   d. How do you determine fund raising goals?
      • Board input?
      • Staff input?
      • Member/Client input?
      • Volunteer input?
      • Community input?

C. HOW IS THE ORGANIZATION PERCEIVED?
   a. Do others understand the mission, goals and objectives?
      View it as a leader?
      • other area not-for-profits and United Way?
      • community leaders not associated with the organiza-
        tion?
      • board and volunteers?
      • parents, alumni and members?
      • staff?
   b. How do you influence the organization's image?
      • What are the media resources in your community?
        – newspapers, radio, television (include "alternative
          media" and minority outreach)
      • What are the community outreach resources?
        – library and church bulletin boards, other not-for-
          profit organizations
      • What are the workplace and company outreach
        vehicles?

- company newsletters, seminars
- How do you communicate with each of the above?
  - ongoing? crisis?
- What outreach events do you schedule?
  - Speaker's Bureau?
  - Focus groups?
  - Recognition events?

II. ORGANIZATIONAL BACKGROUND

A. GENERAL
   a. Define fiscal year: Month ____ to Month ____
   b. Attach organization's history
   c. Attach organizational chart
   d. Attach any strategic plans/documents which provide insight as to upcoming goals/objectives/concerns
   e. Attach Gift Stewardship/Accountability Guidelines (defining who accepts gifts on behalf of the organization, what gifts are acceptable, honoring/recognition processes, etc.)

B. BOARD OF TRUSTEES

   Provide by-laws
   a. Attach list with terms/officers shown.
      Provide biography/resume; include short assessment of "giving/getting" potential.
   b. How is recruitment handled?
      - Nominating process?
      - Terms?
      - Duties?
   c. How is training accomplished?
      - Orientation?
      - Meetings? (schedule/content?)
      - Retreats?
   d. Board chairperson/key members
      - Why are you a part of this organization?
      - How much of your time is spent in networking activities on behalf of the organization?
      - How much of your time is spent in active fund raising?
      - Describe your skills in the following areas:

- Public Speaking
- People Skills
- Fund Raising
  - Technical Background
  - Cultivation/Solicitation
- Where do you feel you need further training?

C. EXECUTIVE DIRECTOR
a. How much of your time is spent in networking activities?
b. How much of your time is spent with United Way?
c. How much of your time is spent in active fund raising?
d. Describe your skills in the following areas:
  - Public Speaking
  - People Skills
  - Fund Raising
    - Technical Background
    - Cultivation/Solicitation
  - Where do you feel you need further training?

III. FUND RAISING

GENERAL QUESTIONS TO CONSIDER:
Overall: what is the case, what are the fund raising goals, what are the financial needs, how strong is your potential market, what investments can be afforded?
- What are the specific programs and needs to be funded this year, next year, and 3–5 years out?
  - How have these needs been determined?
  - How much will they cost?
  - What are the priorities?
  - Have you factored inflation?
- What is the "case" that will be made to donors and prospects? How are you "unique"?
- What is the fund raising goal for this year, next year and for 3–5 years? How have these goals been determined?
  - does this relate to needs?
  - have additional resources been committed (staff, equipment, materials)?
- Where can donations come from and in what amounts: individuals, foundations, corporations, special events, bequests?

**FUND RAISING MEASUREMENTS
TO BE USED**

- $ spent to $ raised in fund raising budget

- % increase of return on the dollar over last time-
  period measured

- increase in donor base

- increase in prospect base

- penetration of new markets

PLANNING CRITERIA
  – are budget constraints managed?
  – are action steps occurring at planned intervals?
  – proposals—number submitted versus number funded
  – is face-to-face contact being maintained with donors,
    prospects, and board?
  – when is planning done?

A. FUND RAISING HISTORY: (for last 3 years if available)
   Attach fund raising budgets

	19—	19—	19—
Fund Raising Income			
Total $ raised	____	____	____
$ raised by category:			
Annual Giving			
• direct mail	____	____	____
• phonathon	____	____	____
• face-to-face	____	____	____
Major Giving	____	____	____
(NOTE: At what level are gifts considered major?)			
Planned Giving			
• realized bequests	____	____	____
• new expectancies	____	____	____

Corporate ___ ___ ___

Foundations ___ ___ ___

Special Events ___ ___ ___

In-Kind (list) ___ ___ ___

- How does this compare with what was budgeted for fund raising income? ___ ___ ___

Fund Raising Expenses
Total $ Spent ___ ___ ___

$ raised by category:
Administrative
- staff ___ ___ ___
- recordkeeping ___ ___ ___
- acknowledgements ___ ___ ___

Annual Giving
- direct mail ___ ___ ___
- phonathon ___ ___ ___
- face-to-face ___ ___ ___

Major Giving ___ ___ ___

Planned Giving
- realized bequests ___ ___ ___
- new expectancies ___ ___ ___

Corporate ___ ___ ___

Foundations ___ ___ ___

Special Events ___ ___ ___

In-Kind (list) ___ ___ ___
- How does this compare with what was budgeted for fund raising expenses? ___ ___ ___

Rate of Return Ratio _ % _ % _ %
(*Total Fund Raising Income over Expense*)

Donor Profile: (for last three years if available)
Attach donor lists. Indicate if Restricted/Unrestricted? How
solicited? Purpose? Donor's relationship to organization?)

	19—	19—	19—
Total Numbers of Donors	____	____	____
Donors by category:			
Annual Giving			
• direct mail	____	____	____
• phonathon	____	____	____
• face-to-face	____	____	____
Major Giving	____	____	____
Planned Giving			
• realized bequests	____	____	____
• new expectancies	____	____	____
Corporate	____	____	____
Foundations	____	____	____
Special Events	____	____	____
In-Kind (list)	____	____	____
Total Prospect Pool	____	____	____
Prospects by category:			
Annual Giving			
• direct mail	____	____	____
• phonathon	____	____	____
• face-to-face	____	____	____
Major Giving	____	____	____

Planned Giving   ____ ____ ____

Corporate   ____ ____ ____

Foundations   ____ ____ ____

B. BOARD GIVING AND GETTING
- Average size of board personal gifts? _____
- Highest gift? _____ Lowest gift? _____
- % of board giving?
- Does board do fund raising? ( ) YES ( ) NO
  How well? How actively? Indicate percentage of time.
- Does board receive fund raising training? How?

C. FUND RAISING STAFFING (for last 3 years if available)

a. #_____ #_____ #_____
Title(s) _____
_____
_____
_____
_____
_____
_____
_____
_____

Attach job description/resumes

b. Attach Organizational/Reporting Chart
  - If you could make changes how would you place the supervisory/reporting relations of Fund Raising/ Membership/Communications? Public Relations?

c. How is the Development Director's time spent?
  (Indicate if you have direct responsibility, supervisory responsibility, or passive involvement)
  - Direct Fund Raising?

 - Face-to-face cultivation and solicitation either on own or with board/staff
 - Fund raising/cultivation events
 - Grantwriting
 - Preparing brochures/letters

- Support Activities?
  - meetings with board, committees, staff
  - report generation
  - data entry
  - recordkeeping
  - gift acknowledgement

- Other Non-Fund Raising Activities? (be specific)

d. For other fund raising and support staff, describe their involvement in:
  - Direct Fund Raising?
    - Face-to-face cultivation and solicitation either on own or with board/staff
    - Fund raising/cultivation events
    - Grantwriting
    - Preparing brochures/letters

  - Support Activities?
    - meetings with board, committees, staff
    - report generation
    - data entry
    - recordkeeping
    - gift acknowledgement

  - Other Non-Fund Raising Activities? (be specific)

e. How does the Development Office interact with the rest of the organization?
  - Do you attend management meetings?
  - Do you attend board meetings?
  - How do you learn about programs?
  - How early do you get information?

f. What types of training and professional growth opportunities exist?
  - Which professional memberships do you have?
  - Which professional meetings do you attend? (regularly, infrequently?)
  - Which training events have you attended in the last three years? Which do you intend to attend in this and next year?
  - Do you have a mentor in fund raising?
  - Do you have a network of fund raising colleagues?

D. FUND RAISING STRATEGY

*Provide a spreadsheet by fiscal year showing all fund raising activities, month by month, for last complete fiscal year. Also a spreadsheet showing completed activities for current year and anticipated activities.

a. General
  - Describe your "typical" donor: who is s/he demographically (age, sex, race, income, marital status, religion, education, profession)? Why does s/he give to your organization? How did s/he learn about your organization?

  - How do you communicate with donors and prospects? Attach any copies available.
    - Annual Report
    - Newsletter
    - Letters from CEO on regular basis
    - Use of PSAs and the media
    - Open Houses
    - Speaker's Bureau

  - Do you have guidelines for Gift Stewardship? How do you determine:
    - What kinds of gifts you accept?
    - At what level may gifts be restricted?
    - What kind of donor acknowledgement and recognition is provided?

- Who at the organization may accept gifts?
- How are in-kind gifts valued internally for recognition?
- How are operating costs and fund raising costs recovered from restricted/endowment gifts?
- What level of funding is required for endowments and scholarships, facility namings, general forms of planned gifts?

- Which general brochures do you have? Attach any copies available.
  - Gift Recognition Levels brochure
  - Bequest Brochure
  - Scholarship Brochure
  - Tribute and Memorial Brochure
  - "Wish List" Brochure (examples of needs)
  - Follow-up Planned-Giving Brochures
  - Corporate Giving Brochure

- Do you use a standard gift reply form? Attach a sample.

b. Gift Acknowledgement/Recognition
  - How do you handle gift acknowledgements? Attach samples of your letters/cards. Are these forms (to what $ cut-off) _____ ? How quickly do these go out to donors ( )within week ( )by 2 weeks ( )longer

  - How accurate is your recordkeeping? How often is updating done? How sophisticated is your system (can you sort by a variety of demographics? Personalize?)

  - What forms of donor recognition do you have?
    - Annual Honor Roll
    - Articles in newsletter
    - Thank-you calls from board, staff
    - Donor Events
    - Donor Clubs
    If you have a donor club tier, attach brochure and/or describe fully

- How do you get donors to join? _____
  _____
- to upgrade? _____
  _____
  _____

c. Annual Fund Raising
  - Look at the past two complete fiscal years:

	19—	**19—**
Total Number of Annual Donors	___	___
Number of Renewing Donors		___
$ From Renewing Donors		___
Number of New Donors		___
$ From New Donors		___

  - What percentage of your annual donors renewed their gifts from the previous fiscal year?
  - What percentage of your annual donors renewed *and* *upgraded* their gifts from the previous fiscal year?
  - What do you see happening with renewal and upgrading in the current year?

  - Do you have an annual giving program with defined timelines, steps? ( ) NO ( ) YES
    - In-person solicitation?
    - Direct Mail Program?
    - Telemarketing Program?
    - United Way? (restrictions on your program?)
    - Matching Gifts Program?

  - What themes, if any, do you use?
    - Early giving
    - End-of-year giving
    - End of fiscal year giving
    - Scholarship appeal
    - Tribute/Memorial giving
    - Facilities needs
    - Crisis appeal

- Do you differentiate between renewal and acquisition fund raising? ( ) NO ( ) YES If yes, how/what?

d. Major (Individual) Gift Fund Raising
  - Do you do prospect research on a regular basis? ( )NO ( )YES: How? _____
    _____
    _____
    _____
    _____

  - Do you have a "hot" list of major giving prospects?
    - Have you developed and rated a significant prospect list—one that makes sense in terms of probably vs. possible interest? ( ) NO ( ) YES

    - Do you have a strategy for moving them along? Describe _____
      _____
      _____
      _____
      _____

    - Are prospect and correspondence files being developed and kept current? ( ) NO ( ) YES

    - Does the board and staff see a sizeable number of potential donors personally? ( ) NO ( ) YES

e. Planned Giving
  - Do you have a planned-giving program ( ) NO ( ) YES If yes,
    - how do you cultivate prospects?
      - brochures
      - advisory council
      - financial planning mailings
      - articles in newsletter
      - mailings
      - advertisements
      - seminars

- visits—who goes?
- recognition

f. Corporate/Foundation Giving
  - Do you do prospect research on a regular basis? ( ) NO ( ) YES How? _____
    _____
    _____
    _____
    _____

  - Do you have a "hot" list of major giving prospects?
    - Have you developed and rated a significant prospect list—one that makes sense in terms of probable vs. possible interest? ( ) NO ( ) YES

    - Do you have a strategy for moving them along? Describe _____
      _____
      _____
      _____
      _____

    - Are prospect and correspondence files being developed and kept current? ( ) NO ( ) YES

    - Does the board and staff see a sizeable number of potential donors personally? ( ) NO ( ) YES

    - Which require grantwriting? How much time does this take? Results?

g. Special Events
  - Do you have a "particular event" or events held each year? ( ) NO ( ) YES—attach description including $$ raised, who attends, # attending, budget, who runs event, etc.

h. Other Fund Raising Income
  - Include any information which might be useful

Fund Raising with a Passion

TARGETED FUND RAISING: *Defining and Refining Your Development Strategy* places its emphasis on demonstrating how to use the fund raising tools and methodologies more effectively and efficiently. However, I'd like to conclude the book with a reminder that "people give to people" and that, without enthusiasm from staff and volunteers, the best methods won't create the miracles we crave.

Recently I attended a luncheon meeting of the Oregon Chapter of the National Society of Fund Raising Executives. The speaker was Martha Sloca Richards, Director of Development at 1000 Friends of Oregon. Martha's rousing talk was inspiring and uplifting. With her permission I am paraphrasing it here for you to read (and reread) when burnout threatens, when no one appreciates you, when you wonder why you decided to be a fund raiser.

PASSION: A DEFINITION

When you feel passionate, you feel intensely about something. Passion is not infatuation; it isn't faddish or fashionable. Passion survives the bumps and grinds of daily contact. It's a long-term commitment and is often blind to imperfections and obstacles. You feel a need to share your interests: to be engaged and to engage others. You feel a compulsion to communicate to others; you cannot hold back your interest and enthusiasm.

Passion: In Our Work

To succeed in fund raising, you must have passion. I submit that successful fund raisers share a passion in common. We believe that we can and should work to improve the human condition. This passion is what motivates you to continue at your job through the long hours, the daily irritations, the countless deadlines, and the squeeze between board, boss, funder, and budget.

Unfortunately, we get divorced from our passions over time. It's easy to be passionate about the job during the first six months to three years when the newness buoys you along. But, it gets tougher as the years accumulate. Habits and patterns are set; you accept the limitations and stop tilting at the windmills.

Without our passions to bolster us, we are worn down by the daily grind. The job becomes tedious; the people we work with and for are too predictable; irritations and conflicts take on larger and larger dimensions. It becomes harder to get moving in the morning; the board meeting looms as an unpleasant task; the coming special event a waste of energy.

Ultimately, when people have not stayed in touch with the passion that brought them into development initially nor sustained and built upon their passion for their agency or organization, they become aimless. Failure to grow your passion will impair your ability to communicate convincingly about your program. It will make it hard for you to place your work in perspective. When passion is forgotten, development directors change agencies after short tenures or leave the profession entirely.

Staying In Touch with Your Passion for Fund Raising

■ **First, find it.** Make time to work on your passion for making a difference. Think about it. Articulate it. Take a minute to explain to a member of your staff or board, a volunteer or a client, even friends or family, what excites you about the organization you work for and/or the program you support.

■ **Then, renew it.** To keep your passion intact, plug back into the energy source which feeds your passion. Talk with the people in your organization and profession who share your passions. Find that new staffer, board member, or volunteer and ask them what attracted them to your organization. Revisit with the "old timer" who shares the stories and still has the energy to be enthusiastic. Talk with your donors and clients and gather the inspirational stories which convey so well why your program is important. Attend presentations by leaders and dreamers you respect and admire and listen to them put in words your passions.

■ **Now, use it.** As you allow your passion to gather strength, you'll communicate better with others. Your voice will be clearer; your eyes brighter. You'll use stronger gestures; look directly at your audience. You'll connect more fully and draw others into your passion.

Using passion elevates your requests above the money, above building projects, above budgets, above the immediate need. It is the passion of staff, board, and volunteers which sets your organization apart and convinces funders they want "in."

Passion rejuvenates and refreshes everyone with whom it comes in contact. Because passion is contagious, it can be the most useful tool you have for motivating yourself and others to work and to give.

A FINAL THOUGHT

Too often, we approach our work as a sprint. It isn't: it's a long-distance marathon. Making a difference requires endurance and ongoing training. Renewing your passion provides you with both the fuel and the skill you will need to place well.

RESOURCE BIBLIOGRAPHY

I drew from a variety of resources in writing *Targeted Fund Raising*. Here is a sampling of those publications and organizations I found especially helpful in compiling the material for this book.

DEMOGRAPHIC AND PSYCHOGRAPHIC RESOURCES

PUBLICATIONS

American Demographics
P.O. Box 68
Ithaca, New York 14851
800/828-1133

If you only buy one publication, this should be it! Each issue of *American Demographics* provides fascinating articles, examples, and statistics on how demographics and psychographics are impacting the American scene. The magazine always references its sources so you can go to the organization that compiled the information or conducted the survey if you desire.

The Boomer Report
FIND/SVP, Inc.
625 Avenue of the Americas
New York, New York 10011
212/645-4500

This monthly newsletter monitors the baby boomer generation—what it's buying, thinking, feeling, and doing next.

The Numbers News
P.O. Box 68
Ithaca, New York 14851
800/828-1133

The Numbers News, a monthly, 12-page newsletter published by American Demographics, Inc., reports the newest facts behind the latest consumer market trends in a quick-read format. Whereas *American Demographics* magazine covers the "big picture," *The Numbers News* concentrates on the numbers behind those consumer trends.

Off the Shelf
2171 Jericho Turnpike
Commack, New York 11725
516/462-2410

Off the Shelf is a bi-monthly free catalog of current market studies industry and company reports, surveys, and other information publications available from leading U.S. and international publishers.

The Public Pulse
205 East Forty-Second Street
New York, New York 10017
212/599-0700

The Public Pulse, published monthly by The Roper Organization, reports what Americans are thinking, doing, and buying. Issues of the newsletter contain a Research Supplement as well.

Research Alert
37-06 30th Avenue
Long Island City, New York 11103
718/626-3356

Research Alert's bi-monthly issues deliver key findings from 10–20 new studies, plus detailed listings of an additional 12–15 new consumer reports. A bonus: many of the reports it identifies offer free or inexpensive copies of their research to the public. They also publish specialized newsletters on the affluent, youth and Hispanic markets.

The Wall Street Journal
420 Lexington Avenue
New York, New York 10170
212/808-6700

Every business day *The Wall Street Journal* provides a wealth of information about consumer marketing trends, research, media choices, and other topics of importance to marketers in its "Marketplace" section.

Yankelovich MONITOR
8 Wright Street
Westport, Connecticut 06880
203/227-2700

The *Yankelovich MONITOR*, launched in 1970, is the longest standing continuing study of social values, attitudes and behavior.

RESEARCH AND REPORTS

The Affluence Explosion: The Real Affluents, The Real Impact
Compiled by Alert Publishing, Inc., New York City 1990

Age Wave
Ken Dychtwald and Joe Flower
Los Angeles: Tarcher, 1989

The 400 Richest People in America
Forbes magazine, October 22, 1990 issue

Success in America: The Cigna Study of the Upper-Affluent
Conducted by Louis Harris and Associates, Inc., New York City, 1987

Workforce 2000
Conducted by the Hudson Institute, New York, 1987

Great Expectations
Landon Y. Jones, New York: Ballantine Books, 1980

Megatrends 2000
John Naisbitt and Patricia Aburdene, New York: William Morrow & Co, 1990

By the Numbers: Using Demographics and Psychographics for Business Growth
Judith E. Nichols, Chicago: Bonus Books, 1990

Successful Marketing to the 50+ Consumer
Jeff Ostroff, New Jersey: Prentice-Hall, 1989

The Chivas Regal Report on Working Americans: Emerging Values for the 1990s
Conducted by Research & Forecasts, New York City, 1989

The Influential Americans
Conducted by the Roper Organization, Inc., October 1989

RESOURCES FOR PHILANTHROPY, DEVELOPMENT AND FUND RAISING

American Association of Fund Raising Counsel
   Trust for Philanthropy (publishers of *Giving USA*)
25 West 43 Street
New York, NY 10036
212/354-5799

The Chronicle of Philanthropy
1255 Twenty-third Street, NW
Washington, DC 20037
202/466-1200

The Foundation Center (publishers of *The Foundation News*)
79 Fifth Avenue
New York, NY 10003
800/424-9836

Fund Raising Management magazine
224 Seventh Street
Garden City, NY 11530
212/516-6700

Independent Sector
1928 L Street, NW, Suite 1201
Washington DC 20036
202/223-8100

The National Society of Fund Raising Executives
1101 King Street, Suite 3000
Alexandria, VA 22314
703/684-0410

The Heritage Collection is a collection of books NSFRE feels has contributed significantly to the body of knowledge in fund raising. Available through NSFRE, they include:

American Association of Fund Raising Counsel, GIVING USA

Ashton, Debra, THE COMPLETE GUIDE TO PLANNED GIVING

Balthaser, William F., CALL FOR HELP

Barnes, David W., THE FUND RAISERS PLANNING & BUDGETING GUIDE

Bremner, Robert, AMERICAN PHILANTHROPY

Berendt, Robert & J. Richard Taft, HOW TO RATE YOUR DEVELOPMENT OFFICE

Brakeley, George A., TESTED WAYS TO SUCCESS-FUL FUND RAISING

Broce, Thomas E., FUND RAISING: A GUIDE TO RAISING MONEY FROM PRIVATE SOURCES

Cohen, Lilly & Young, Dennis, CAREER FOR DREAMERS AND DOERS

Dannelley, Paul, FUND RAISING AND PUBLIC RE-LATIONS

Fink, Norman S. & Metzler, Howard, THE COSTS AND BENEFITS OF DEFERRED GIVING

Flanagan, Joan, THE GRASSROOTS FUND RAISING BOOK

Franklin, Benjamin, AUTOBIOGRAPHY AND OTHER WRITINGS

Fund Raising Institute, FRI PROSPECT-RESEARCH RESOURCE

Grasty, William K. & Sheinkopt, Kenneth, SUCCESS-FUL FUND RAISING

Gurin, Maurice, WHAT VOLUNTEERS SHOULD KNOW FOR SUCCESSFUL FUND RAISING

Hodgkinson, Virginia A. & Weitzman, Murray S., DIMENSIONS OF THE INDEPENDENT SECTOR

Hopkins, Bruce G., CHARITY UNDER SIEGE

Huntsinger, Jerald E., FUND RAISING LETTERS

King, George V., DEFERRED GIFTS: HOW TO GET THEM

Kiritz, Norton J., PROGRAM PLANNING & PROPOSAL WRITING

Jenkins, Jeanne B. & Lucas, Marilyn, HOW TO FIND PHILANTHROPIC DOLLARS

Kotler, Philip, MARKETING FOR NON-PROFIT ORGANIZATIONS

Lautman, Kay & Goldstein, Henry, DEAR FRIEND: MASTERING THE ART OF DIRECT MAIL FUND RAISING

Layton, Daphne Noibe, PHILANTHROPY AND VOLUNTEERISM: AN ANNOTATED BIBLIOGRAPHY

Lord, James Gregory, PHILANTHROPY AND MARKETING

Luck, Michael F. & Tolle, Donald J., COMMUNITY COLLEGE DEVELOPMENT

Nichols, Judith E., CHANGING DEMOGRAPHICS: FUND RAISING IN THE 1990s

Non-Profit Network, THE INTERNATIONAL CERTIFICATE IN FUND RAISING VIDEOTAPES

O'Connell, Brian, AMERICA'S VOLUNTARY SPIRIT

O'Connell, Brian, PHILANTHROPHY IN ACTION

O'Connell, Brian, THE BOARD MEMBER'S BOOK

Panas, Jerold, MEGA GIFTS: WHO GIVES THEM, WHO GETS THEM

Podesta, Aldo C., RAISING FUNDS FROM AMERICA'S 2,000,000 OVERLOOKED CORPORATIONS

Raybin, Arthur, HOW TO HIRE THE RIGHT FUND RAISING CONSULTANT

Semple, Lisa, PULLING THE DESK BOOK FOR FUND RAISERS

Seymour, Harold J., DESIGNS FOR FUND RAISING

Sharpe, Robert F., THE PLANNED GIVING IDEA BOOK

Stuhr, Robert L., ON DEVELOPMENT

Tatum, Liston, COMPUTER BOOK FOR FUND RAISERS

Warner, Irving, THE ART OF FUND RAISING

Whitcomb, Nike B., MONEY MAKERS

The NonProfit Times
P.O. Box 408
Hopewell, NY 08525
609-466-4600

Public Management Institute (publishers of
The Corporate 500)
358 Brannan Street
San Francisco, CA 94107
415/896-1900

Ms. Nichols' books are available through Pluribus Press. For ordering information call toll-free 1-800-225-3775.

CHANGING DEMOGRAPHICS:
Fund Raising in the 1990s
   March 1990   267 pages $34.95

A 1990 selection for the National Society of Fund Raising Executives' Heritage Collection. A lively, candid discussion on understanding and reaching the donor groups of the 1990s. Written specifically for fund raisers, CHANGING DEMOGRAPHICS offers practical advice for targeting baby boomers, baby busters, Hispanic-Americans, older Americans, and working women. Each aspect of development strategies— annual giving, major and planned giving, corporate and foundation relations, and volunteerism—is discussed demographically and psychographically.

BY THE NUMBERS:
Using Demographics and Psychographics for Business Growth in the 1990s
   September 1990   300 pages $24.95

A true "how to" book, filled with practical advice on marketing strategies every organization can use to reach baby boomers, aging America, the Hispanic majority, working women, and baby busters. Recommended for not-for-profits concerned with attracting members, clients, and customers for their services, BY THE NUMBERS describes the "hot" niches for the 1990s—health, education, financial planning, leisure, and the home. Also discussed: how demographic change will affect the leadership and workforce of the 1990s.

ABOUT THE AUTHOR

Judith E. Nichols, author of *Changing Demographics: Fund Raising in the 1990s* and *By the Numbers: Using Demographics and Psychographics for Business Growth in the 1990s,* (Pluribus Press, 1990), is an independent marketing consultant and lecturer who specializes in helping organizations understand changing demographics.

Her articles and workshops have brought her national recognition. She has spoken at numerous national and regional meetings of the Council for the Advancement and Support of Education (CASE), international conferences, and chapter meetings of the National Society of Fund Raising Executives (NSFRE).

Among the not-for-profit organizations she has worked with are: the American Heart Association, the American Lung Association, the American Red Cross, Boys and Girls Clubs of America, Boy Scouts of America, Campfire Inc., Girl Scouts of the USA, the National Association of Independent Schools (NAIS), the National Catholic Development Conference, the National Resource Council for Community Colleges (NRCC), Planned Parenthood Federation, United Way, and the YMCA.

A senior certified fund raiser, Ms. Nichols served as Vice President for Development at Portland State University, Oregon; and headed development efforts at Wayne State University, Detroit, and the New Jersey Institute of Technology. She has worked extensively with the YMCAs as well as a number of cultural, membership, health, and social service organizations. Her development program at Wayne State received the silver medal for "Most Improved Development Program of the Decade" from CASE.

An active member of the National Society of Fund Raising Executives, Ms. Nichols has served on both the Michigan and Oregon boards.